Introduction

This book is a compilation of unique mandalas, based on a collection of designs by Asheville Mandala Weavers and offering inspiration for mandala makers of all abilities.

I have always been inspired to create – several years ago I trained under a master in the field of mandala making. My teacher, now retired, was Jay Mohler and this book would not exist without his dedication and hard work in teaching me and my colleagues over the years. This unique art form has inspired many across the globe to connect with their longings and create something that they can look at that represents something bigger in their life. Mandalas are story tellers. They paint a picture with weaving that inspires us to have strength, courage, hope and joy in life. Jay is a master, and my friend, who dedicated his life to this art form. I am truly inspired and grateful to represent this art and bring the beauty and skills I have learned from him to the world. My gift is to carry out his workmanship and this art, helping others to explore the beauty of the mandalas.

As without, so within.

May this work help you to embody the art of the mandala by utilizing the skills of weaving, meditation and your own inner life to bring a unique piece of art into the world while connecting and improving your own wellbeing.

This book is designed for beginners but also includes some slightly more advanced instructions, providing you with a variety of techniques. Each mandala builds on the previous one,, giving you the opportunity to develop your skills and to create mandalas ranging from basic to more intricate designs. My hope is that these offerings will assist you in developing the skills needed to make your own personal creations, while also bringing you mindful moments to help you strengthen your inner commitment to internal growth.

Mandala designs and patterns are unique to each of us, and creativity will lead you and guide you in the process of making your own personal work. This often happens as new patterns and designs emerge from within you. Colors are also a unique way to make something your own. I often look for what inspires me in the natural world, furniture or a simple blanket design. All can provide inspiration for your own creation.

My hope is that with hard work, dedication and commitment to your craft you will grow in the art of weaving, learning this rewarding skill and feeling a sense of joy and wonder as you create.

Inga Savage

Tools and Materials

Here is a look at the tools and materials used to make the mandalas in this book – it feels like a great place to get started! I'll also cover some tips in my Mindful Moments that will help with creativity and meditative focus, as well as showing you how to fine tune your skills.

ESSENTIAL TOOLS

One of the great things about mandala making is that the equipment you will need is easy to source and relatively inexpensive. You will probably find that you have most of the tools already in your household toolkit. Read the notes in this section and refer to the photograph below to make sure you have everything you need to hand before you begin. Using these tools to prepare a bunch of dowels ahead of time is my favorite way to roll with inspiration – it makes sitting down and immediately exploring my ideas easy. So assemble your tools and get some dowels ready to roll (see *Getting Started: Preparing the Dowels*) so you can instantly respond to those sweet inspiring moments.

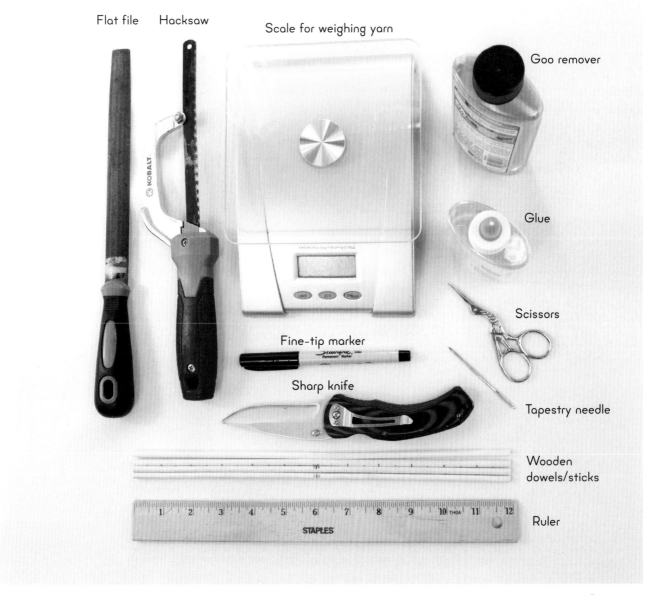

Flat file   Hacksaw   Scale for weighing yarn   Goo remover

Glue

Scissors

Fine-tip marker   Tapestry needle

Sharp knife

Wooden dowels/sticks

Ruler

HARDWARE

First on my list is the wood I choose (see *Choosing Dowels*), but carefully chosen tools will also help to make your weaving a pleasure and a success.

HACKSAW

For a beginner the hacksaw is a perfect hand-held saw that allows control and precision when cutting a dowel down to size. When cutting, the hacksaw should be held in your dominant hand, with the other hand firmly holding the stick. I usually hold one end on a hard surface with the end I am cutting poking off the edge. Then I make a cut close to the hard surface, but not so close as to damage it, to saw the dowel in two.

TOOLS FOR MEASURING AND MARKING

I use either a tape measure or a flat ruler for measuring dowels and spacing the markings on them (see *Preparing the Dowels*). On the whole I prefer to use a ruler, and stick with that to ensure consistency. Don't switch from one measuring method to another. Use a marker pen to mark your measurements. These can be any color you like, but I tend to use black as it's easy to see. For different sections of markings I sometimes use different colors – this is a personal choice but can be helpful if you are going to use multiple colors in the sections of your design and want to mark them.

FILES

After you have measured and marked you will need a flat or triangular file to make notches. My preferred tool is a flat file. If you take a look at a flat file like the one shown in the photograph, you'll see that the front of the file is flat and the back is rounded. I prefer this type of file over the triangle for several reasons. I love the sensation in my hands – it has a better feel for me when I hold it, as opposed to the smaller triangle files. I use a triangle file for small projects that need more precision and detail and the flat rounded for larger projects. When filing I like to press the flat side of the file on the stick with the round side facing toward me. After making countless mandalas, I find this the most comfortable way to work with it.

BOX CUTTER, KNIFE OR CHISEL

These tools can be used when carving out the center notch that allows two dowels to nest together (see *Preparing the Dowels*). I mostly use a knife like the one pictured in the *Essential Tools* photograph.

GLUE

Use glue for the ends of the mandala so the yarn does not slip off the sticks after you have finished weaving. I don't usually glue anything else. You might find you need 'goo remover' and a rag for those pesky stickers the department store puts on the sticks for pricing. I really do not like weaving with sticky dowels, so this removes mess and leaves your sticks with a smooth surface worth holding and spinning in your hands.

CHOOSING YARN

I recommend worsted weight (aran) yarn, either 100% wool or acrylic. I don't recommend cotton yarn as it will stretch over time. It is not necessary to stick with using one type of yarn – they can be mixed as you choose. Novelty yarns such as glitter tinsel or ones with beads can be useful in small quantities to accent the design of the mandala.

I buy my yarn from a variety of places, from natural wool suppliers to my local yarn or craft shops and online stores. Some of the big craft stores carry suitable weight yarn that can be used for your mandala in a wide range of synthetic and wool varieties. Several brands of acrylic yarn come in many brilliant colors and are relatively inexpensive, which can prove to be great for the novice or beginner.

Online vendors also carry a large variety of suitable yarns. Brands such as Cascade 220 and KnitPicks' Wool of the Andes are my favorites, along with many other higher-end brands (see *Suppliers* for details). Each artist develops a feel and preference for the yarn as they learn and grow. I also like to spin and dye my own yarn, which gives a wonderful fine texture that then can be double-plied.

FINDING INSPIRATION

I derive inspiration from many different things: nature, a life situation, a season. I recommend you find what inspires you! Research online to find some inspiration to get you started.

COLOR CONSIDERATIONS

Selecting a color range is very important in driving the design of your mandala. There are two different basic ways of choosing colors: the first is to select gradients of similar colors that fade into one another, and the second is to pick very different yet complementary colors. Incorporating both of these techniques when choosing colors will ensure a beautiful and harmonious color palette. If you are feeling uneasy about picking colors, consult an online color wheel or search for 'color inspiration'. These methods have proven to inspire me to start imagining what can be created. I sometimes even look at paint swatches to get a color combination. Many things can inspire you – let yourself be stretched and just go for it.

I recommend a correlation between the size of mandala and the number of colors you integrate into your design: the larger the mandala, the more colors you can use. For example, if you are making a 12in (30cm) mandala, you'll probably want six to eight colors at most. For a larger mandala, say 24in (61cm), you may want to use as many as 12–14 different colors. Of course, each mandala is different. Sometimes a very large mandala will use very few colors. Generally, though, you won't want to use too many colors on a small design, as it can feel very busy and that isn't what we want for our meditative mandalas.

YARN QUANTITIES

Now let's briefly look at how much yarn you might need for different sized mandalas. The amounts below are general estimates. Everyone will use slightly more or less yarn and some will have more waste than others, but if you follow this guide I think you will have enough. As you get into the larger mandalas you will need to plan to use whole skeins of yarn and just be grateful when you have leftovers. For now my suggestion is this:

Mandala Size	Amount of Yarn used
12 x 12in (30 x 30cm)	6–8oz (175–225g)
14 x 14in (35.5 x 35.5cm)	10oz (280g)
16 x 16in (40.5 x 40.5cm)	15oz (425g)
18 x 18in (46 x 46cm)	20oz (550g)

CHOOSING DOWELS

Bear in mind that as the size of mandala you are making increases, so the dowel diameter must increase too. This is to avoid breakages as much as possible, although despite our best efforts sometimes our dowels do break – it happens to me, even as a skilled weaver! If this happens regularly when you are weaving, think about using a size bigger.

Another way to avoid breakages is to be mindful of tension (see *A Note about Tension*) and don't notch your dowels too deeply. Tension has a way of building up so that suddenly you'll find your dowels are warped, and the slightest movement may break them. This takes practice to notice, but with time you will learn to catch this quickly and become a master of tension.

CHOOSING THE RIGHT SIZE

Below is a list I use to determine the proper gauge of dowels you will need for each size of mandala. If you are new to weaving mandalas, I would recommend that you go small – it helps to practice on easy-to-handle sticks when you are developing your skills and confidence in your weaving.

Dowel Size	Mandala Size
$1/16$ or $3/16$in (2 or 4mm)	12in (30cm) to 14in (35.5cm)
$1/4$in (6mm)	up to 16in (40.5cm)
$5/16$in (8mm)	up to 22in (56cm)
$3/8$in (1cm)	up to 32in (81cm)
$7/16$in (1.25cm)	up to 40in (101cm)

A NOTE ABOUT TENSION

If you tend to pull the yarn very tightly when you weave, your sticks may bend or even break. If that's the case, go up one size in your dowels.

MY RECOMMENDATIONS

Poplar and oak dowels are my preferred choice for 36in (91cm) and 48in (122cm) lengths. For larger mandalas, such as 24in (61cm) or more, oak dowels are a safe choice as the wood is harder and stronger than poplar or a blend. Poplar and blended woods are softer and tend to break more easily on larger mandalas, but work fine for smaller ones of up to 18in (46cm) in diameter. These are suitable for small mandalas and ornaments.

BUYING YOUR DOWELS

Dowels can be purchased at craft stores often in packs containing around twelve $1/16$in (2mm) gauge dowels. Some stores sell this size in boxes of 100 dowels. In hardware stores you'll find individual 36-38in (91-96.5cm) long dowels that can be cut down to size. Buying online is another option, but the problem I run into here is that I can't physically hold them and check them for bends. At times dowels can bow when wet, so I prefer to buy sticks in person when possible to avoid getting warped sticks (1). This becomes increasingly important with larger pieces.

Consider the number of sides and the size of the mandala you will be making in order to purchase the correct number of dowels. For example, if you are making a four-sided, 12in (30cm) mandala you will need two poplar or oak dowels, 12in (30cm) each. For small eight-sided mandalas, using pre-cut poplar sticks is best. For an 18in (46cm) eight-sided mandala, you will need four 18in (46cm) oak dowels. You will therefore need to purchase two 36in (92cm) dowels and cut each one in half.

Inspect the dowels before you buy to ensure there are no obvious bends or cracks in them. I recommend purchasing one or two extra dowels just in case one breaks once you get started.

1

HOW TO BEGIN –
SETTING AN INTENTION

Making mandalas is all about balance and centering, mentally and physically. It's important to stay focused on all the elements of the mandala – the colors, the evenness, the spacing, etc. – throughout the entire creative process to ensure you produce a professional-looking mandala.

Don't be afraid to unwind and start over. It may take a few tries to get the tension just right, or maybe the color you added changed the overall feel of the mandala in a way that was not to your liking. Making art is a process: unwind and start over again until it's just right for you!

Now set an intention to start the mandala. Intentions are specific desires and longings – look into yourself for what you want to create more of in your life. As you set this intention begin with longing or a desire. It may sound something like 'I intend to create more joy, peace and happiness'. Then expand on that and say something like 'by opening up to all the possibilities and making space for myself to receive that joy or happiness'. Then write that intention down on a piece of paper and place it near to where you will begin to weave. Be open to more inspiration that may come to you as you weave.

Getting Started

We will start with the basics: directions for four-sided mandalas, and then some steps for multi-sided mandala making. In this first chapter you'll learn how to make the cross at the center of every mandala, how to wrap the dowels, and how to consider tension and change colors. Let's begin!

PREPARING THE DOWELS

To begin, you will need to cut your dowels to the length you desire. It is more than likely that you will have purchased longer lengths than you actually want to work with, so the first step is to carefully measure and mark the dowel, then cut it down to size. I often measure a minimum of two times end to end to make sure that I have not accidentally slightly moved my sticks. At every stage of the dowel preparation process, it is important that you measure your sticks against one another to ensure that they are all the same length. I will go over this in more detail when I discuss marking the sticks.

HOW TO MARK AND CUT THE DOWELS

1. Measure from one end to the middle of each stick to find the center, and mark it. Repeat from the other end. It's important to measure from both ends to ensure that you have a true center. If you're working on an 12in (30cm) mandala, for example, measure to 6in (15cm), mark it, flip the stick and measure to 6in (15cm) again and make a second mark. If the marks are the same, it means your stick is exactly 12in (30cm). This will rarely be the case, so be sure you measure from both ends on every single dowel and at every step of the process. Put an X or a cross at this center mark to distinguish it from the rest of the marks that follow (1).

2. Next, measure and mark every half inch and whole inch (1.25cm and 2.5cm), starting from each end towards the center mark. Every half inch, make a small vertical mark. Every inch, make a longer vertical mark (2). As with finding the center of the dowel, the accuracy of your measured marks is less important than making sure that your sticks match one another perfectly. To that end, it works best to use one dowel as your 'master' stick; measure and mark it first and then use that (rather than the ruler) to mark each successive stick. This will help ensure symmetry from the very beginning of the process.

3. After you have marked all your dowels, you will need to make a small 'notch box' around the center mark that measures slightly less than the width of the dowel. For example, if you are using a ¼in (6mm) dowel, you should mark a box that is roughly ³⁄₁₆in (4mm) in diameter around the center mark. For half your dowels, make the center notch box on the same side of the dowel as the half-inch and inch markings. For the other half of your sticks, make this center notch box on the unmarked side of the dowel (3). The reason for this is that when you put two dowels together into a cross, these center notches will fit together to better hold the cross shape in place, and you'll be able to see your marks on both sticks.

4. Cut very shallow grooves at either end of the box and a third towards the center, using a knife. Don't cut too deeply, or you risk weakening your dowel too much, which can cause it to break. Next use your chisel, box cutter, or some other knife to pop out the notch at the center (4).

5. Next, gently bend each of the dowels to check its strength. To be sure that you haven't cut too deeply, it is very important that you test-bend your sticks before moving on. It is far better to break a dowel in the preparation phase than after you have spent hours weaving on it!

6. File notches every inch (2.5cm) of the dowels by placing one of the triangular file's edges vertically against your longer vertical marks and filing a shallow groove (5). These grooves help ensure that the yarn will not slip or bunch up as you work and will aid in the overall symmetry and longevity of the mandala. Don't cut them too deep or, as with the center notches, you run the risk of weakening your sticks.

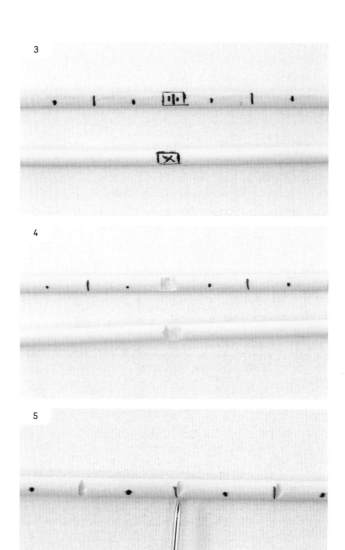

CREATING THE
FIRST CENTER

This is the starting point for making a four-sided mandala, or the first of two or more centers if you are making a multi-sided mandala.

1. Start by setting your intention (see *How to Begin – Setting an Intention*), then hold two dowels together in your non-dominant hand, one with the center mark on the same side as the guide marks and the other with the center mark on the opposite side to the marks. Place the dowels together so that they are perpendicular to each other and all the guide marks face you. If you followed the instructions in *Preparing the Dowels,* you will have carved a notch so that they interlock. Now we are going to put them together at that intersection. You can glue the two dowels together if you'd like but it's not necessary as they will be stable enough after just a few wraps of yarn.

2. With your first color yarn (I've used a dark color in these photos so the yarn is easy to see), place the end of the yarn across the point where the dowels cross, fold the yarn end over as shown and hold it with a finger so that the tail is pointing down at the back and the remainder of the yarn is hanging down at the front (1).

3. Holding everything together (sticks and yarn) between your thumb and a finger, begin wrapping the yarn with your dominant hand, starting with the dowel pointing toward 6 o'clock position (see tip). Wrap once clockwise around this arm (2). This will always be the bottom-most or 'first' stick of your mandala. If necessary, make a mark on the dowel so that you remember this, as you'll want to keep track of how many times you weave completely around the mandala throughout the creation process to ensure that all sides stay even.

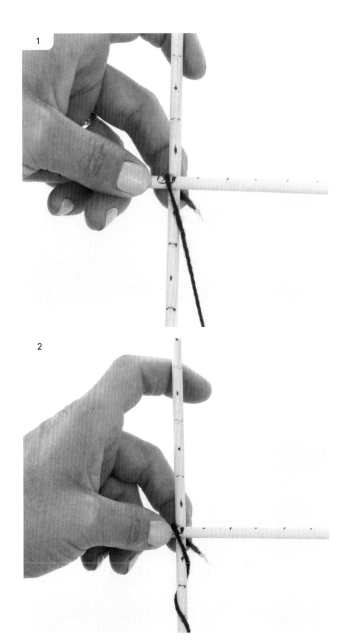

Throughout this book you will note that I refer to the position of the sticks as '6 o'clock' or '3 o'clock' etc. Just picture the face of a normal analogue clock to see which stick is being referred to.

3

4. Carry the yarn out and to the right, to the dowel arm facing 3 o'clock (you will be moving in a counter-clockwise motion), pass the yarn over the top of the dowel and wrap it clockwise around that arm.

MOVE ONE WAY, BUT WRAP THE OTHER

To be clear, you will move from one arm to the next in a counter-clockwise motion. However, you will wrap the yarn around each individual arm in a clockwise motion.

5. Continue to the 12 o'clock dowel and then the 9 o'clock dowel, wrapping each one clockwise in the same fashion until you get back to your first wrapped arm (3).

6. Once you get back to the first arm, begin wrapping the yarn twice around each arm clockwise to create a nice even space for each strand of yarn (4). Remember to place each string just next to the previous one and avoid overlapping. I also recommend gently pushing the yarn you have wrapped up toward the center to ensure that each wrap is flush against the one before it. Between each circuit around the dowels, check that the dowel ends remain equidistant from each other.

7. Continue to wrap the dowels in your first color. It is important to manage the tension of your yarn as you make each wrap. Not too tight, not too loose. If it's too tight, you'll notice the dowels start to bend significantly and you'll risk them breaking and losing all your beautiful work. If it's too loose, your yarn will sag and the dowels will not hold their place (see *Tension*).

4

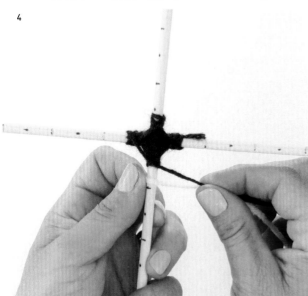

CREATING A DOUBLE CENTER

For an eight-sided mandala you will need two centers, each on a separate set of sticks. The second center is almost always larger than the first center – my rule of thumb is that it should be one wrap bigger. When you finish the first center (see *Creating the First Center*), end with a temporary knot so that after you have completed the second center you can secure your next yarn without any unraveling.

The next step is to join the two centers together, which can be a bit tricky. I recommend using either the dagger or diamond pattern when joining the centers. This allows them to be secured firmly but still allows some adjustability if you haven't mastered the art of keeping the dowel arms equidistant from each other as you work.

HOLDING THE CENTERS TOGETHER

To start, put the first center in your left hand between your forefinger and thumb (use your right hand if you are left-handed). With the color you will use for the next pattern, use the color change technique (see *Changing Colors*) to secure the yarn, then place the second center behind the first one, holding it in your last three fingers so that you have both parts of the mandala in one hand (1). Check that the sticks are arranged so there is an equal gap between the stick ends.

JOINING WITH DAGGERS

For this you will need to follow the instructions for the dagger pattern (see *Insight: Daggers*), but this time you'll use it to join the mandala together. This method is actually just as straightforward as making a simple dagger, except that there are two sets of sticks to hold.

1. When you have the centers securely in your hand (see *Holding the Centers Together*), take the dagger yarn to the right under the first three sticks. Bring the yarn up to the right of the fourth stick, come over the top of that stick and wrap around it twice (2). You can see how a dagger holds the two centers together if you flip the mandala over to look at the back (3).

2. Take the yarn under the next three sticks, then wrap it twice around the stick that you started on to complete the first dagger (4).

3. Repeat to make the required number of dagger wraps. Tie off with a simple knot. At this point check the 'arrows' that the dagger forms and adjust them if necessary into a precise 'v'-like pattern to make them neat. Most designs will require you to make another set of daggers on each stick, or possibly just on a pair of sticks. When you have completed all the daggers, the two centers will be secure and you can start the next design element.

JOINING WITH THE DIAMOND PATTERN

For this you will need to follow the instructions for the diamond pattern (see *Retro Vintage: Diamond Pattern*). The diamond is very similar to the square pattern you will find in the four-sided mandalas chapter, except this time you need to skip under a stick; this creates the diamond.

1. When you are holding the centers securely in your hand (see *Holding the Centers Together*) and have secured your yarn on the stick in the 6 o'clock position (this will be part of the top set of sticks), take the yarn in a counter-clockwise direction, going under the back set of sticks (5).

2. Come up on the left side of the top set of sticks, taking the yarn over the top of the next stick and wrapping it twice as usual (6).

3. Keeping the distance equal between the sticks, take the yarn under the next stick in the back set of sticks and secure it to the next top stick, wrapping twice. From there take the yarn under the next back stick and over to the next top stick, wrapping it twice. Continue in this way to make the first diamond pattern pass and attach the two centers together. Repeat as many passes as your design requires, checking the distance between the sticks as you change color (7).

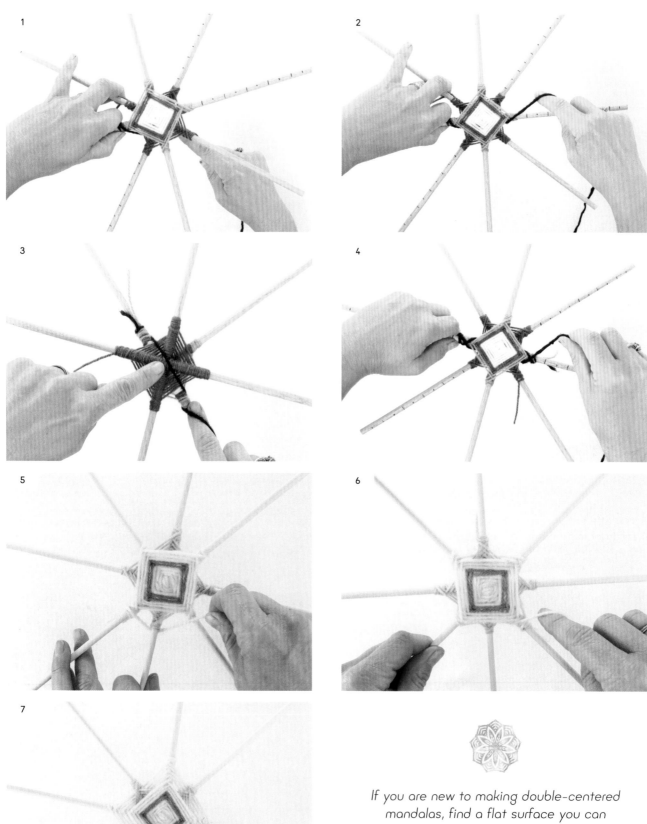

If you are new to making double-centered mandalas, find a flat surface you can slide and spin the mandala on while joining the centers, then you don't need to stress about holding the mandala.

TENSION

Wrapping the yarn tight, but not too tight, as you move from arm to arm is something to be aware of throughout your creation. We will continue to visit this skill often as this holds great importance as you move outward from the center of the mandala.

* Wrapping too tightly will cause your dowels to bend inward or back as you move further toward the edge. Wrapping too loosely will cause the yarn to sag. As you move from arm to arm, keeping one finger over the yarn that you just wrapped, tug gently as you wrap the yarn around the next arm.

* Be sure to check regularly that the dowels are still equidistant from each other. Doing this often will alleviate many issues later on and is worth the effort. You can never check the spacing of the dowels too much! I recommend measuring the spacing between the end of each dowel after every color change and making adjustments as needed and often. Although it's impossible to be perfect, you want to try to make them as close to exact as possible. For example, on an eight-sided, 12in (30cm) mandala the tips of the dowels should sit 4½in (11.5cm) apart. Tension can often throw this off, causing one stick to be pulled too close to another, and then the symmetry of the mandala will be off.

* Catching problems with your tension early on will help you create a more symmetrical and appealing mandala, so the effort is worth it in the end. Keep trying and if you need to unwind, do it. It's ok! Practice makes perfect.

Mindful Moment

Tension in wrapping your mandalas is really a practice of patience and care. Making sure the yarn is tight enough and not too tight is like having balance and harmony in your life. Being either too rigid or having no boundaries can lead to problems.

CHANGING COLORS

If you would like to change colors, continue wrapping a circuit until you reach the first arm again. For a 12in (30cm) mandala, I recommend not going much past the first 1in (2.5cm) notch on the dowels while creating the eye, or center diamond, to ensure a well-balanced mandala.

1. When you are ready to change colors at any phase of the mandala, cut your original piece of yarn, leaving a tail of about 1in (2.5cm) from the last dowel that you intend to wrap it around.

2. With the mandala in one hand, hold the original piece of yarn beside the dowel you are ending on and place the new and old yarns together (1).

3. Flip the mandala over, holding both pieces of yarn, and twirl the old and new yarns together tightly (2).

4. Wrap the new yarn around the dowel and *over* the hanging tails of yarn to secure them against the dowel (3), and continue on with your design in the new color, dropping the old color as you make the second turn around the stick (4). Don't forget to check your tension after each color change (see *Tension*).

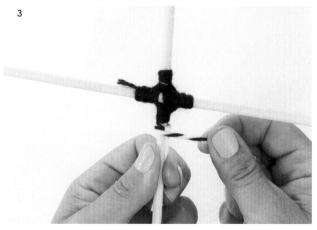

I recommend using the color changing technique to start any new yarn. As you finish with one yarn, tie it in a loose knot around the nearest dowel, so that your weaving doesn't unravel. When you need to start a new yarn on that stick, undo the knot and use the color changing method to get going again.

Four-sided
Mandalas

Insight

In this particular mandala I went with a dark center, which I very rarely do, but since I almost always start with white, I feel it's important to address the fact that this time, I didn't. Sometimes the dark center makes a statement. For me it is not about avoiding it, it's just about knowing when to use it. I use a dark center when the effect needs to be simple and not distract from the overall pattern. Because this mandala is small, it is a nice point of focus.

YOU WILL NEED

Two wooden dowels, 12in (30cm) long and ³⁄₁₆in (4mm) in diameter

Worsted-weight (aran) yarn, 6oz (175g) of each of the following colors: dark purple, light purple, cream, light green, orange, yellow, and black

Worsted-weight (aran) yarn, 3oz (85g) of white

Essential tools (see *Tools and Materials*)

Finished size: 12 x 12in (30 x 30cm)

INSIGHT

1. See *Getting Started: Preparing the Dowels* to mark and notch your sticks so you're ready to begin wrapping. OK, let's start with the center eye. Following the instructions in *Getting Started: Creating the First Center*, start with dark purple and wrap in a counter-clockwise pattern. Wrap once around each dowel to secure them in place. Then on the second round start wrapping twice around each stick for a total of five circuits.

2. Once you have gone around each stick five times you need to make a color change to white (see *Getting Started: Changing Colors*), and complete one circuit round all the sticks (1). Next switch to the light purple and make three passes on all four sticks. Change to the dark purple yarn and do two rounds of that. Next switch to cream to do two passes around all the sticks and follow with two light green (2). You are now ready for the next design feature: daggers (3).

1

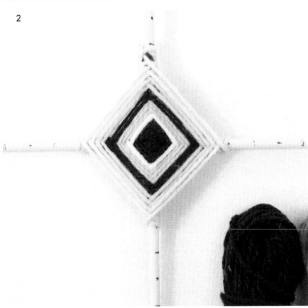

2

Mindful Moment

The dagger is my favorite way to stabilize sticks and strengthen the structure of a mandala. Paying careful attention here to tension will give you a more stable base to work on. This is also true in life. Sometimes closely observing the detail of our lives can give insight into what needs attention. Don't be afraid to spend a little extra time on the details. It's worth it, and so are you.

DAGGERS

Daggers are a design element that creates negative space within the mandala and allows you to add small pops of color. It is also one of the techniques I recommend when your design includes attaching more than one center together (see *Getting Started: Creating a Double Center*).

3. Starting with any dowel, wrap the dark purple yarn twice around the dowel (3), then take the yarn behind the mandala to the dowel opposite it (4) and wrap twice around that stick in the clockwise fashion we discussed earlier (5).

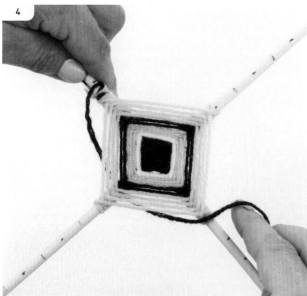

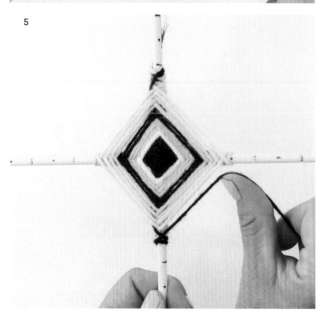

4. Next bring the yarn behind the mandala back to where you started on the first dowel, and wrap again in a clockwise fashion (6). Do this with the dark purple yarn twice, forming two 'arrows' or daggers. The reverse shows how the yarn passes between the opposite sticks (7).

5. As you switch to add this element to another pair of dowels you can just cut the yarn, leaving a tail of about an inch (2.5cm), and tie it off on the dowel with a simple knot until you are ready to add more yarn to it. Be sure to add the dagger design to all the dowels before you move on to the next color.

6. When you have completed this on both sets of sticks in dark purple, switch to the orange yarn and do two daggers on each pair of sticks (8), then move to yellow and do four daggers on each set of sticks. This completes your first set of daggers.

6

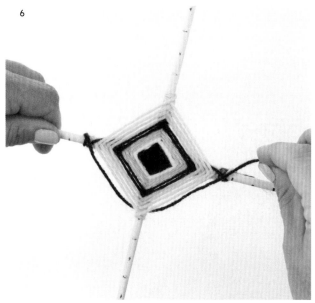

7

8

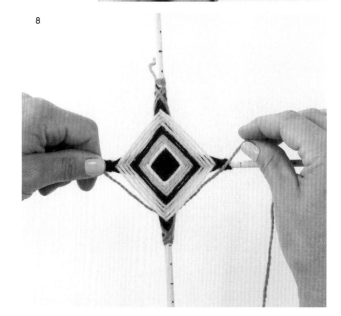

Mindful Moment

One thing to notice at this time is that making space for placing each yarn can become a point of focus. Use this mindful moment to pause and breathe deeply. Is your yarn overlapping in any area? Do you need to unwind and redo anything? Are the sticks equally spaced or did one pull out of place? This is the time to notice, to observe, and to start to pay attention. Practice, practice, practice.

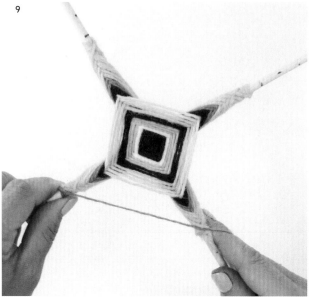

INNER SQUARE

7. Using the same technique as the one for making the center, we are now going to create a square pattern. Starting from one of the dagger strings, undo the simple knot you finished the dagger with and proceed with a color change using the light purple yarn (9). Make a square by going round each stick in a counter-clockwise fashion, wrapping each stick twice (10). Make three complete passes around all four sticks.

8. Next, switch to white yarn and make one complete pass, then change to orange and make four passes, then switch to black to accent with one pass. Then change colors again and make four complete passes around each stick in light green, making sure to wrap each stick twice. Then change color to do two complete rounds around all four sticks in black before switching to the light purple for your final color for this section. Use the light purple to make three complete passes. You have now completed your first square. Make a simple knot to secure the yarn. Check the spacing between your sticks (see *Getting Started: Tension*).

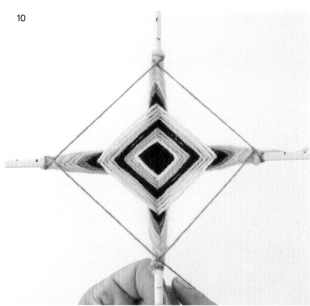

SECOND DAGGERS

9. Pick up where you finished the light purple square and switch colors to the dark purple yarn. Use the method described above (see *Daggers*) to complete daggers on both pairs of sticks with two passes of dark purple yarn. Then switch colors again to the light purple yarn to make two more pairs of daggers to complete this section.

OUTER SQUARE

10. Finish your mandala by making another square, starting with one of the dagger yarn ends and changing the color to light green yarn. Make three complete squares around the mandala, then switch to dark purple and make one complete square. Next, switch to orange and make two complete squares before doing two more in yellow. Finally, switch to light purple for three complete squares, then do two light green ones and finish with one orange square. You're done – great job! Secure all your ends and prepare to hang up your mandala (see *General Techniques: Finishing the Mandala*).

Blue Horizon

Once again I have not chosen white for the eye of this mandala, but instead I selected a soft gray. I find that making this adjustment helps me 'feel' my way into color changing more easily, as well as making me focus on color gradients. Attention to the subtle changes around us and within us plays such an important role in our daily life too…This mandala is embellished with tassels, providing another chance to pick up a color from within the design that either subtly tones or introduces a bright contrast.

YOU WILL NEED

Two wooden dowels, 12in (30cm) long and 1⁄16in (2mm) in diameter

Worsted-weight (aran) yarn, 6oz (175g) of each of the following colors: light gray, dark green, light green, light blue, baby blue, red, purple, yellow, and variegated light blue

Essential tools (see *Tools and Materials*)

Finished size: 12 x 12in (30 x 30cm)

BLUE HORIZON

CENTER

1. Follow the instructions in *Getting Started: Preparing the Dowels* to mark and notch your sticks, then see *Getting Started: Creating the First Center* so you're ready to create the center of your mandala. With light gray yarn, wrap in a counter-clockwise pattern using a clockwise motion over each stick. Wrap once around each stick to secure them in place. Then on the second round, wrap twice around each stick for a total of five passes.

2. Now you are ready to change color. Place the new dark green and old gray yarns together and follow the instructions in *Getting Started: Changing Colors* to continue the wrap. Make two passes round the four sticks in dark green.

3. Make another color change and complete two passes of light blue yarn, then switch to light green and make two passes of that on all four sticks. When complete, change to the light blue make two passes, then and finally do two rounds of baby blue (1). You are now ready for the next element of this design.

FIRST DAGGERS

4. For the first set of daggers make four passes of red yarn, then one pass with dark green (see *Insight: Daggers* for how to create this element). Next make a highlight dagger of light green with one pass around the sticks, and finish off this dagger with three turns of purple yarn (2). When you have completed the dagger section, take a breath. Remember to be mindful and take this time to make sure your arrows are straight (3). I use a small needle to line up my arrows so that they are as perfect as possible. If your tension is off (see *Getting Started: Tension*), unwrap the yarn and start over – practice makes perfect!

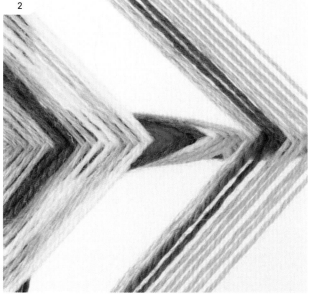

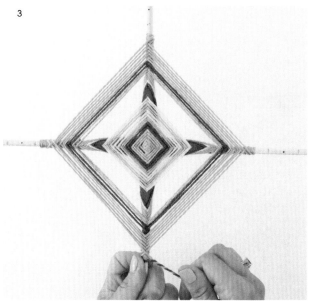

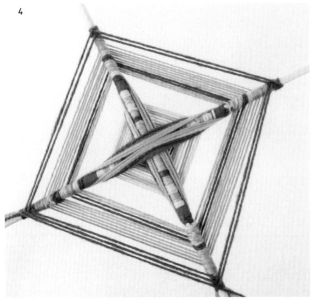

INNER SQUARE

5. For the next section, start with the light gray yarn that you used in the center. Make two passes round the sticks, then switch to dark green and make two more passes. Next, I made one pass of gray as an accent, or you could use the light green. I then made five turns with the purple yarn.

6. For the final three passes of dark green I added an accent by flipping the mandala over and working from the reverse side, instead of weaving on the top of the sticks – deviating from the traditional square technique to add extra dimension (4). This is a nice subtle change that can be used for more advanced work, but is simple and easy to do (5). I've shown you this only as a suggestion – you may play around with what pattern best suits you. If you prefer structure and repetition, you can work the square from the front.

SECOND DAGGERS

7. For the next part of this mandala we will make a second set of daggers (see *Insight: Daggers*), starting with two passes over each stick with red, then changing color to yellow and making more three passes (6).

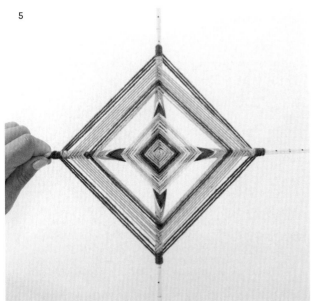

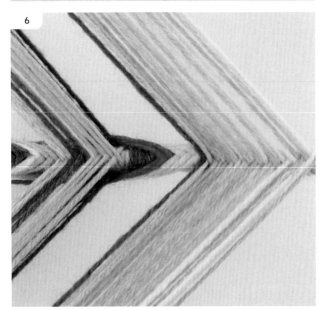

Mindful Moment

Our perspective on life and change can be gentle and forgiving, just like the color changes in this mandala. You can develop more compassion and patience as you observe these subtle aspects, and then learn to adjust and make different choices, not from a place of judgment or harshness but from softness.

OUTER SQUARE

8. Complete the mandala using a square pattern. I started with the dark green to accent this. I made one dark green pass, then two light green passes before moving to a variegated light blue yarn that is so subtle in this mandala that its color changes are hardly noticeable. However, if you're looking for inspiration for how to bring your mandala together at the end, a yarn like this can unite the colors and give the mandala perfect harmony. To finish the square I made about 12 passes of the variegated colored yarn and one of dark green (7). Weave in your yarn ends and glue them (see *General Techniques: Finishing the Mandala*).

INTEGRATED TASSELS

Several of the mandalas in this book are embellished with tassels. Some hang on strings, but these ones are tied into the mandala. Here is how I make them.

9. Find a small book that is about a hand's width wide on its shortest side, or a 4in (10cm) wide rectangle of stiff card, and wrap your chosen yarn (for the Blue Horizon mandala I chose red and yellow) around it about 20 times. Snip the middle of the yarn to make lengths of about 4in (10cm), then wrap one length of yarn twice round the mid-point of the lengths of yarn and tie a knot (8).

10. Next, take the knotting yarn and thread each end through the mandala from front to back, to either side of one of the sticks, as shown (9). In the case of the Blue Horizon mandala I threaded it between the dark green yarn on the inner edge of the square pattern and the next light green yarn. You can thread the string onto a tapestry needle to make the next steps easier.

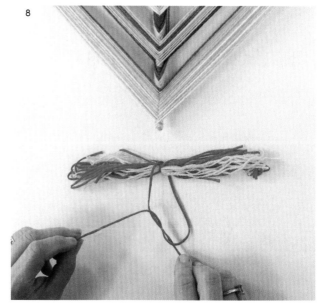

Mindful Moment

It is good to observe where we need attention to skill and detail. Do not be afraid to observe, deconstruct, and redo. That is how we become masterful in our life.

11. Flip the mandala over and tie a knot (10). Then bring one end of the yarn back through to the front, at a point about one-third of the way in from the outside edge of the mandala, then repeat with the other end of the yarn (11).

12. Flip the mandala back over so that the front is facing you, then with one string now on the right, cross the yarns in the front of the mandala over each other about one-third of the way down the tassel to create a pom-pom effect (12).

13. Take the yarn back on either side and thread it through the same spot it came up through, then tie it off (13). Then flip the mandala over and trim the tassel to create a nice tidy finish. Repeat this technique for the other tassels to complete the mandala.

Earth and Fire

This mandala uses the same techniques as the previous one, but here I played with earth and fire colors to show how they really work together. Using the idea of these elements I began weaving with the softness of the center eye and finished with some simple embroidery. I hope you will enjoy playing with colors and thinking about this brief introduction to theme.

YOU WILL NEED

Two wooden dowels, 12in (30cm) long and ³⁄₁₆in (4mm) in diameter

Worsted-weight (aran) yarn, 6oz (175g) of each of the following colors: white, dark green, light green, red, black, and medium green

Essential tools (see *Tools and Materials*)

Finished size: 12 x 12in (30 x 30cm)

EARTH AND FIRE

CENTER

1. Let us begin with our two dowels marked, cut and ready to go (see *Getting Started: Preparing the Dowels*). Follow the instructions in *Getting Started: Creating the First Center*, to begin this mandala with white yarn for the center. Make six passes to complete the center, then change color to dark green to make one pass (see *Getting Started: Changing Colors*). After that, make another color change to light green, complete four passes of that, then color change to do one outline in white. This completes the center (1).

INNER DAGGERS

2. For instructions on creating this element, see *Insight: Daggers*. To begin, make a color change, switching from white to dark green. Next create the daggers with four wraps of the dark green yarn, four light green wraps, and four wraps of red yarn (2).

INNER SQUARE

3. For the next section, outline the daggers with a square (see *Insight: Inner Square*). Do this using a color change to start, then make two passes of dark green, followed by three passes of light green. To finish, change to black to make one more pass.

OUTER DAGGERS

4. To create the next section of daggers, make a color change and start with three wraps of the light green yarn. Then make another color change and do two medium green wraps, followed by a final outlining with a single wrap of white. This completed the daggers for this mandala (3).

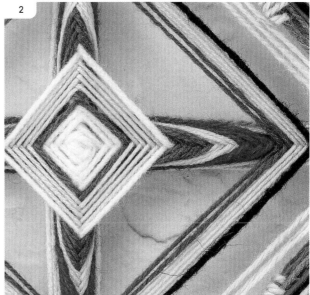

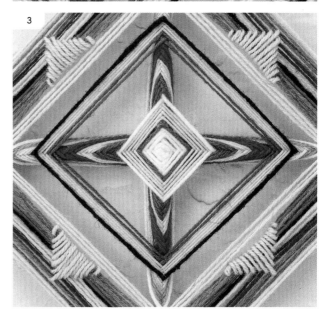

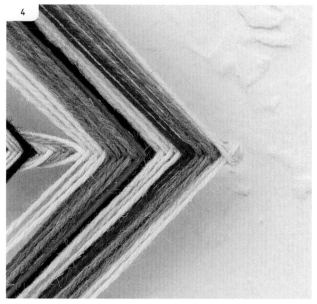

OUTER SQUARE

5. To finish, I chose to do a large outer square to create a bigger area. This allows for tassels or embroidery to add extra dimension to the mandala. Start this square with a color change to the light green yarn. Make three passes, then change to medium green for four more passes. Next change to red for one pass of the yarn – this allows for a really fiery pop of color.

6. Outline the red with a color change to black for one pass, then change to light green to make two passes, and then to dark green for two more passes. I then chose the medium green to pull the depth back into the mandala, so make four passes in this color. Finish the outer square with a color change back to light green and make two passes. This completes the basic shape of the mandala (4). Weave in your yarn ends and glue them (see *General Techniques: Finishing the Mandala*).

TRIANGLE EMBROIDERY

8. Embroidery can add an extra dimension to your mandalas, and is simple to work (see *General Techniques: Adding Embroidery*). For this mandala I chose a simple stitched pattern that I call the triangle embroidery. Using light green yarn in your tapestry needle, start from the reverse of the mandala and follow the diagram (6) to see where to bring your needle through the strings of the mandala's outer square (5). Weave the ends of your embroidery yarn into the reverse of the mandala to secure them.

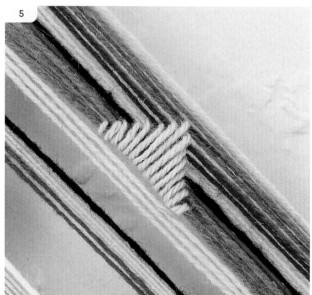

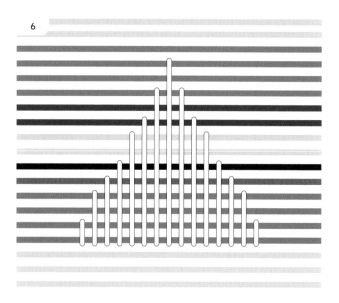

If you made a stitch too long or short, or if you need to join your yarn while weaving the mandala, for example if a string breaks, it's ok. The triangle pattern is very forgiving and can cover those natural mistakes so that no one will never know.

Peaceful Light

I have included this mandala for the unique embroidery that accents its simple design, making it radiate beauty. If you are not up for the embroidery challenge, the mandala alone is stunning and can be left without embellishment, or you can choose a simpler embroidery design such as the versatile squares patterns I've used on the Sage Brush and Star Bright mandalas. But if you like a challenge, please try the design here - it really is worth it!

YOU WILL NEED

Two wooden dowels, 12in (30cm) long and ³⁄₁₆in (4mm) in diameter

Worsted-weight (aran) yarn, 6oz (175g) of each of the following colors: white, dark green, light green, dark brown, light tan, yellow, and purple

Essential tools (see *Tools and Materials*)

Finished size: 12 x 12in (30 x 30cm)

PEACEFUL LIGHT

CENTER

1. Let's begin with a traditional white center. As I have said before, white is the most common color for the center and gives it a clean brightness. Mark and notch your dowels (see *Getting Started: Preparing the Dowels*) and follow the instructions in *Getting Started: Creating the First Center* to start the center. Make six complete passes round the sticks with the white yarn.

2. Next make a color change to dark green (see *Getting Started: Changing Color*). Make two passes in dark green, then change to white for two passes, change to light green for two more passes, and finish the center square with one pass of white yarn (1).

INNER DAGGERS

3. Now you are ready to start creating some daggers (see *Insight: Daggers* for instructions on this technique). Starting with any dowel, make daggers with three wraps of the dark brown yarn. When you have completed this on both sets of sticks, switch to white for one dagger on one set of sticks, then change to light tan and do three more passes.

4. Then switch to the opposite set of dowels, make the highlight white dagger again and finish with three passes of light tan. You have now completed the inner daggers for this mandala (2).

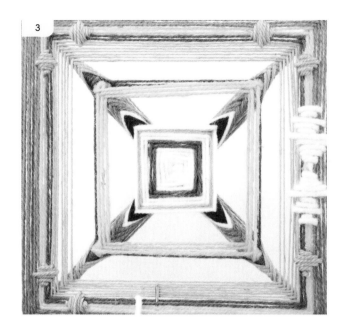

INNER SQUARE AND OUTER DAGGERS

5. Next make three passes of yellow in a counter-clockwise fashion to create another square. Flip the mandala over then, working on the reverse, color change to dark green and make two passes. Working on the back of the mandala creates the space and depth needed for the final purple dagger.

6. After creating the green square on the back of the mandala, change to purple and make a dagger with three passes of the yarn on each stick (3).

OUTER SQUARE

7. The final square is done with seven passes of light green, then two of dark green, two of yellow, and ten of light tan, finishing with two passes of dark brown. This section can vary depending on your weaving tension. Your mandala may only need eight or may need 12 passes of tan. Just do what is needed so as to leave enough space for the two passes of dark brown. Weave in your yarn ends and glue them (see *General Techniques: Finishing the Mandala*).

Mindful Moment

Flexibility is what is required in the outer square. If you need to make a few extra wraps to take up the slack or lose a few to fit, just do what is feels right (not what I say!). The only importance is to have enough space for two dark brown passes to finish. So be flexible, life is more enjoyable when we allow for space to give and take, and the mandala has a life of its own! What does it need?

EMBROIDERY

Once you have completed the basic design, you can begin the embroidery (see *General Techniques: Adding Embroidery*). If you are new to embroidery, why not set this mandala aside and try a simple technique for practice, such as the triangle embroidery in the Earth and Fire mandala? You can always come back to this one at a later date. However, if you like a challenge – go for it! The directions may feel daunting but the reward is amazing, as the addition of embroidery to this little mandala really makes it pop.

8. First we are going to create the purple embroidered diamond shapes. Referring to the photograph (4), start from the left-hand side of the diamond and increase each stitch until you make the fourth one the longest, then step the stitch size back down again. Weave the yarn ends into the back of each diamond as you complete it. Finishing a small embroidery can cause some stress if you pull too tight, so be careful to not add too much tension when tidying the ends. Repeat this embroidery near the dowels on all four sides of the mandala as shown, making a total of eight diamonds.

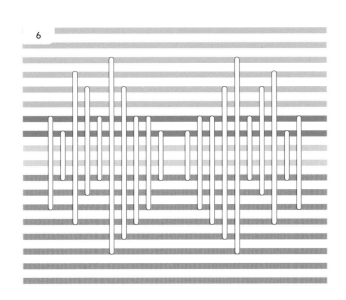

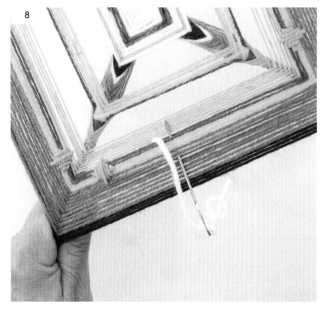

9. For the central pattern you will need your tapestry needle and a strand of white yarn 36in (90cm) in length. Start from the back of the mandala and push the needle through to the front (5). Follow the diagram (6) and take a close look at the photograph (7). Remember to make sure you watch the tension and boundaries for your lines of embroidery. This is the art of practice not perfection.

9. Make the stitches as shown (8, 9, 10) until you reach the central stitch of the pattern. Note that to complete the other side of the embroidery you just need to repeat the stitches in reverse order (see diagram). Work this white embroidery on all four sides of the mandala.

10. To secure the yarn tails, flip the mandala over and weave the loose ends into the embroidery pattern. I weave in my yarn tails on the back of the mandala so as to keep the strings tucked and neat. Do not pull too tight as this will make the last stitch hard to see and distort the design. This completes the embroidery. I hope you found the challenge rewarding and can see how it brings both depth and interest to the mandala.

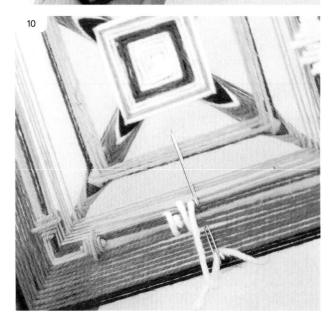

Mindful Moment

When making mandalas, I like to try to feel my way into the patterns and designs before I start to weave. Something to keep in mind is flexibility – you may suddenly feel the need to embroider or add tassels to your mandala. Follow your inner wisdom, engage in the art of playing with a design, and let yourself feel what is required.

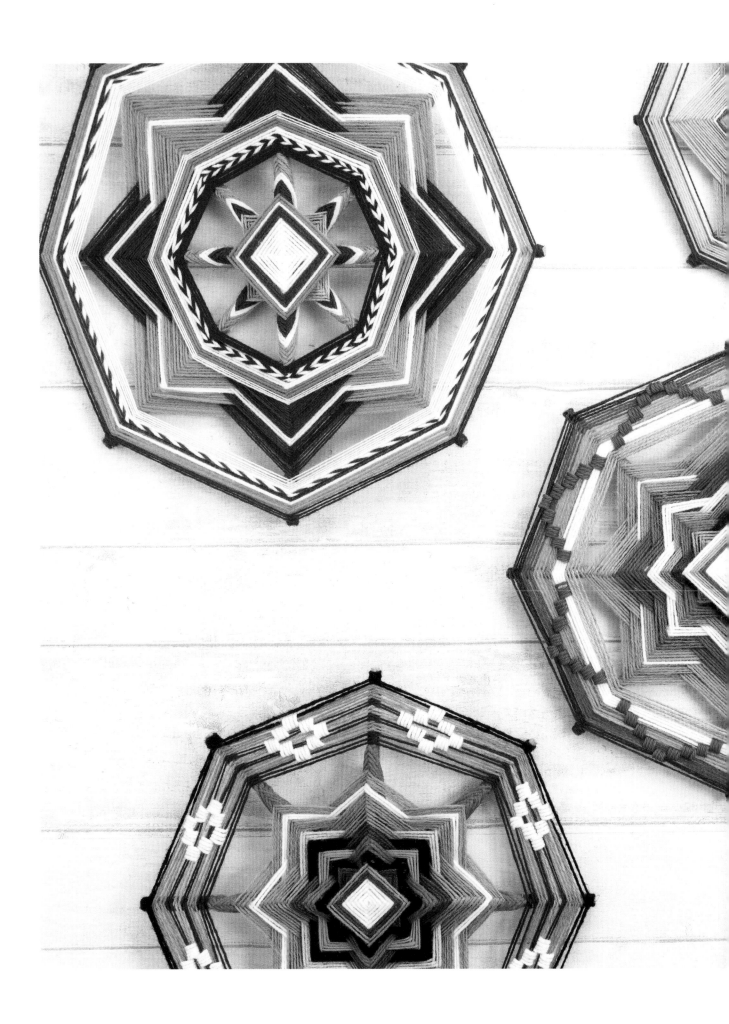

Multi - sided
Mandalas

Retro Vintage

This is the first mandala in this book that has two centers, and uses four dowels to make an intricate star-shaped outline. I like the challenge of finding something new to stretch my skills. Tea-dyeing one of the yarns for this mandala was one such technique, which opened a door for a fun experiment in dyeing! There are whole books dedicated to the wonder of wool and the artistry of what you can do with it, which you might like to explore. Or simply buy three tones of yarn to make this softly colored vintage-style mandala.

YOU WILL NEED

Four wooden dowels, 12in (30cm) long and 1⁄16in (2mm) in diameter

Worsted-weight (aran) yarn, 6oz (175g) of each of the following colors: off-white, camel brown, and beige (tea-dyed or just purchased)

Essential tools (see *Tools and Materials*)

Finished size: 12 x 12in (30 x 30cm)

CENTER

1. Note that this is a double center, so once you have marked and notched the four sticks (see *Getting Started: Preparing the Dowels*), follow the instructions in *Getting Started: Creating a Double Center*. The first eye will start with two sticks and the off-white yarn. I chose this soft color because it suits the retro vintage style of this mandala. Start with five complete passes round the sticks, then make a color change to camel brown (see *Getting Started: Changing Colors*) and make two passes round the sticks. Next make three more passes with the off-white yarn, then set this first center to one side.

2. Start the next eye using the other two sticks and the beige tea-dyed yarn. This will be the underneath eye. Wrap once around each stick to secure the sticks in place, as usual, then on the second round wrap twice around each stick 12 times. It is now time to join the two centers. If this is your first attempt at this, have patience and remember: practice not perfection. This step can be tricky, but following the method described in *Getting Started: Creating a Double Center – Joining with the Diamond Pattern* will secure the centers while allowing some adjustability, which will help if your sticks aren't quite equidistant from each other.

DIAMOND PATTERN

3. For this mandala we will use the diamond pattern to hold the centers together. Secure the off-white yarn to one of the front sticks, then holding the sticks firmly, wrap the yarn in a counter-clockwise fashion, going under the back set of sticks and wrapping twice round each of the top set of sticks in the usual way.

4. Repeat step 3 to make four passes with the off-white yarn, each time going under the back sticks and wrapping twice round each front stick. The structure will become more secure with each pass and you will begin to see how it holds together.

5. After checking the tension with the sticks and making sure they are equally spaced at about 1¾in (4.5cm), start with the 4 o'clock stick and the beige yarn and resume the same diamond pattern you used in steps 3 and 4. Work counter-clockwise under the front sticks and over the back ones, continuing for four passes (1). The needle in the image is pointing to the arrow. You can use your needle to arrange the v shape in each dagger to make it look more clean.

6. For the next diamond pattern, change your yarn to the beige color. Start with three beige passes, then change to camel brown and make one pass.

Make the time to create your own yarn color. Take white yarn, let it sit in vinegar overnight and then squeeze it out. Next apply heavily steeped tea that is warm or cool. Let the yarn sit overnight, then rinse and dry it and you're done.

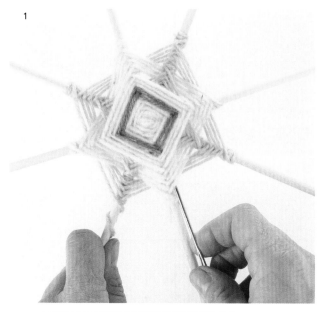

7. Then move to the back set of sticks to create a diamond pattern in off-white with four passes (2).

8. Now move back to the front set of sticks and do three beige passes in the same diamond pattern, followed by three passes of beige on the back sticks. Next, outline these beige diamonds with two passes of off-white yarn on the top set of sticks and then two more on the back set of sticks, to add a soft highlight to the mandala.

9. We will now add a fourth set of diamonds. Starting with the 6 o'clock stick, secure the camel brown yarn and make four passes round the front set of sticks, going under the back set as before. When complete, move to the rear set of sticks and make five off-white passes (3). This is one wrap more than the top set of sticks – I needed an extra wrap because the yarn I used was a slightly different texture to the others. You can gauge this and use your judgment based on the texture of the yarn you use.

Mindful Moment

I notice in life that when things are out of balance it is usually a good time to pause and breathe, to check that I am neither overdoing it nor letting things slide. Finding the sweet spot between tension and alignment between the front and back sets of sticks in the mandala is a lot like that. So let's make sure now that we are aligned and balanced.

10. Continue to wrap the diamond patterns in the following order to finish the mandala: camel brown for four passes on the front sticks, off-white yarn for five passes on the back sticks, beige yarn for five passes on the front sticks, off-white for five passes on the back sticks, beige for five passes on the top sticks, then five passes of off-white on the back sticks. Create a border for the last two sets of diamonds by making two passes with the camel yarn on the front sticks, and then the same on the back sticks. To finish off, add five passes in off-white on the front sticks, then five on the back sticks, and edge the mandala with a border in camel by making three or four passes (depending on your tension) on the front sticks and the same on the back sticks (4).

11. Weave in your yarn ends and glue them (see *General Techniques: Finishing the Mandala*) before adding the hanging tassels.

4

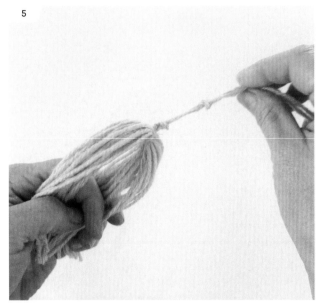

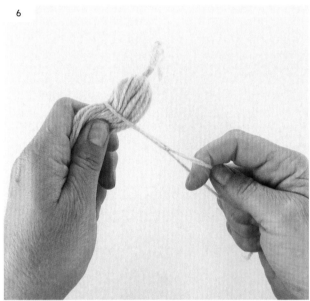

HANGING TASSELS

The making of these tassels begins in the same way as those described in the Blue Horizon mandala (see *Blue Horizon: Integrated Tassels*), but they are attached by longer strings so they hang down, and this affects the way they are tied.

12. For these tassels, I started with about 20 wraps around my book (or a 4in/10cm card); if you want thinner tassels you can make fewer wraps. I used a 12in (30cm) string to tie the center of the tassel, leaving the extra string on the top to attach to the mandala.

13. At this point these tassels differ from the Blue Horizon ones. Tie one knot in the string that was used to split the tassel, close to the strands that will make the tassel, and then another knot about 1in (2.5cm) further up the string, as shown (5).

14. Next tie the 'bulb' of the tassel with another 12in (30cm) string (6), and trim the ends.

15. Tidy the ends of the tassel with scissors (7), then repeat to make a total of two beige tassels and one in camel brown yarn.

16. Secure the tassels to the mandala by tying the yarn to the back of the three lowest sticks, as shown in the main photograph. Congratulations on completing the Vintage Retro mandala – you did a fantastic job!

Pure and Simple

In this eight-sided mandala, we will again be starting with a double center, but this time I am going to show you how to join the centers with daggers. They create a light, open space around the central focus as well as adding a pop of red color that is continued harmoniously in a diamond pattern and in the outer circle. I like using negative space to open up possibilities. With larger mandalas, this space also helps to draw the eye into the center. It helps me remember that we are all connected.

YOU WILL NEED

Four wooden dowels, 12in (30cm) long and 1/16in (2mm) in diameter

Worsted-weight (aran) yarn, 6oz (175g) of each of the following colors: white, dark teal, pale green, mid blue, off-white, red, camel, light teal, light blue and dark red

Essential tools (see *Tools and Materials*)

Finished size: 12 x 12in (30 x 30cm)

CENTER

1. This mandala has a double center, so once you have marked and notched your four sticks (see *Getting Started: Preparing the Dowels*), follow the instructions in *Getting Started: Creating a Double Center*. To begin the first center, make four passes with white yarn in a counter-clockwise fashion. Then make a color change (see *Getting Started: Changing Colors*) to make one dark teal wrap on each stick, followed by another three of pale green. Change to white yarn again to make one more wrap around each stick, ending this with a simple knot to allow you to come back to it after the second center is complete without any unraveling.

2. The second center, which goes behind the first one, is a dark teal color. For this center, wrap your yarn 12 times around the next pair of dowels. Then cut the string and create a simple knot to tie it off (1).

DAGGERS

3. Once you have completed both your centers, it's time to join them together (for details, see *Getting Started: Creating a Double Center – Joining with Daggers*). With the first center in your non-dominant hand, make a color change from white to mid blue yarn, then place the second center behind the first. Make three dagger wraps on one stick, tying off with a simple knot, before proceeding to the next stick. Make three daggers on all the sticks in mid blue, then repeat with three in pale green, three in red, and two in camel (2). Make sure you complete all the daggers in each color before doing the color changes to the next, to keep the central star pattern clean and neat.

When you start a new section, try to begin with a stick that has a knot tying off a previous yarn and secure the new yarn with the color change technique. I like to start like this, as it reduces the excess yarn at the back of the mandala and keeps your loose ends tidy.

CIRCLE PATTERN

4. Next we will do a circle pattern by going from stick to stick in a counter-clockwise fashion, wrapping each stick twice to secure the yarn. Make a color change to light teal yarn and do two passes of the circle pattern. Change to dark teal for one pass, then make one more pass with the off-white, wrapping each stick twice as you go to complete the inner circle (3).

DIAMOND PATTERN

5. The diamond section is the largest part of this mandala. See *Retro Vintage: Diamond Pattern* for detailed instructions on this technique. I chose bright colors to off-set the center pattern. Starting with the top set of sticks at the 6 o'clock position, make a color change to light blue, then go under the stick to the right and over the second stick, continuing to make four passes in this color. Then change to dark teal for one pass and off-white for one more to create an outline. Tie off with a simple knot.

6. Move on to the next set of sticks to start the opposite diamond pattern, this time in dark red, and make five passes before adding an outline with one pass of off-white yarn.

7. Next make a color change, or tie a new string on, and continue with the light teal color to make three passes on the top four sticks, then three passes on the back sticks in camel yarn. Repeat the light teal and camel diamonds three more times for a total of four light teal and four camel diamonds. This completes the diamond section of the mandala (4).

When you have completed the first pass of the circle, check that the distance from stick to stick is equal before doing another pass. Once the circle is in place the sticks move a lot less so, if not re-adjusted, the mandala can look distorted.

OUTER CIRCLE

8. Start on any stick, again working in a clockwise fashion, to make one pass in dark red, followed by a color change and one pass in off-white yarn over each stick. Then take the dark teal and, making another color change, do one pass over each stick. Change again to light teal and do five complete passes over every stick.

9. For the outer edge, make a color change to dark red for one pass and to light teal for one more. Change to dark red again and complete the mandala with three passes around the circle (5). If at the very outside of the mandala you have any exposed dowel, do another pass or two over each stick till everything is covered. Sometimes I have to use my judgment, and depending on how tightly I wove the mandala, I may need to add one more round or make one less.

10. Tie off and weave the end into the back of the mandala, then glue the ends of the dowels to avoid unraveling (see *General Techniques: Finishing the Mandala*).

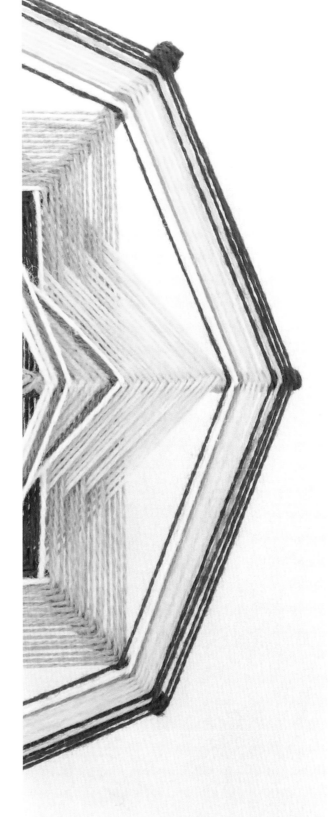

Mindful Moment

When tying off or doing color changes I like to keep my yarn cut short so as to make transitions neat. This helps in life also. Not holding onto things for too long and learning to keep things in the present moment will help you to not hold a grudge and to move forward in life. Let it go and be done with it.

Little Gem

This is another great easy pattern for beginners to start weaving, and offers another opportunity to practice making daggers and the circle and diamond patterns. I chose to make this a slightly larger design to allow for the space that the daggers need. The new technique you will learn here is the twist pattern that creates a herringbone effect. There's a trick to getting this right, so read on to find out how to add this to your mastered skills.

YOU WILL NEED

Four wooden dowels, 16in (40.5cm) long and ¼in (6mm) in diameter

Worsted-weight (aran) yarn, 15oz (425g) of each of the following colors: white, soft purple, teal, light blue, burgundy, green, and bright purple

Essential tools (see *Tools and Materials*)

Finished size: 16 x 16in (40.5 x 40.5cm)

LITTLE GEM

CENTER

1. Follow the instructions in *Getting Started: Preparing the Dowels* to mark and notch your sticks, then see *Getting Started: Creating a Double Center* for how to begin. The first center will use two sticks and the white yarn. Start by weaving eight rounds in a counter-clockwise fashion, then make a color change (see *Getting Started: Changing Colors*) to the soft purple yarn for three passes, before changing back to white for one pass. Finish the first center with two passes of teal yarn. If you want to check by counting, this will be a total of 14 passes. Make a simple knot in the end of the yarn and set the first center aside.

2. Next pick up the remaining set of sticks (these will be the back sticks) and start the second center with light blue yarn. Make 15 passes in the light blue to complete the back center.

DAGGERS

3. Now move on to attaching the two centers together with daggers (see *Getting Started: Creating a Double Center – Joining with Daggers*). To secure the sticks, make a color change to burgundy and then do three dagger passes, starting with the top set of sticks. Switch to the back set of sticks to make the same burgundy daggers there too. Then move back to the top set of sticks, make a color change to white, and do two dagger passes. Change color to green and complete the daggers on the top sticks with four passes of the yarn. Switch to the back set of sticks, make a color change and do two dagger passes of white, then change color and do four green passes. When you have completed all the daggers, pause and check their alignment (1).

Mindful Moment.

I like to align my daggers at this point, prior to starting the circle. I use a needle to make sure the dagger arrows point perfectly outward from the center. This is important for a sharp look. When we pay attention to our own center, we are more able to serve others. As with the mandala, a strong center will support the rest. Take time to adjust your daggers – it's worth it.

CIRCLE PATTERN
WITH HERRINGBONE

4. Start the circle with three rounds of bright purple yarn (see *Pure and Simple: Circle Pattern*). Do not cut the yarn, but add the white, twisting the yarns clockwise together as if doing a color change and wrapping around the starting stick twice to secure the white and the bright purple (2); note that this photo and the next one show the twisting of the yarn for the outer circle, but the technique is exactly the same. Check that the distance between each of the sticks is about 4½in (11.5cm) before going on.

5. Keep twisting the yarns together until you have enough to span the length between the sticks. Then move counter-clockwise to the next stick and wrap the stick twice (3). Continuing to twist the yarn, move counter-clockwise to the next stick and wrap that stick twice. Repeat to complete the circle once all the way around. Check the distance between the sticks again. It is easy to pull the sticks out of balance because you are so focused on the twist.

6. At this point you need to unwind enough of the two balls of yarn to make the next pass of the circle *prior to* reversing the twist – this will help keep the yarn from curling up in a mixed-up mess and causing frustration! Now you've sorted out your yarn, go back to the mandala and get ready to twist the yarn in the reverse direction. I take my time doing this as it takes some care to form a herringbone effect.

7. Twist the white and bright purple yarns together as before, but counter-clockwise to reverse the twist. Line up the colors as you work and move in a counter-clockwise fashion to create the herringbone pattern (4).

8. When you are done, cut the bright purple yarn but not the white, then continue making a circle in a counter-clockwise direction until you have made two passes in white. Color change to teal do three passes in the same counter-clockwise direction, then make three more passes in light blue, still in the same direction. This will complete the inner circle pattern (5). When you are done, finish with a simple knot.

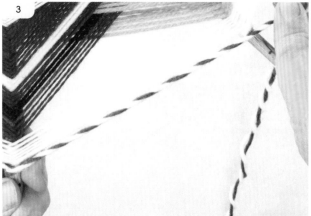

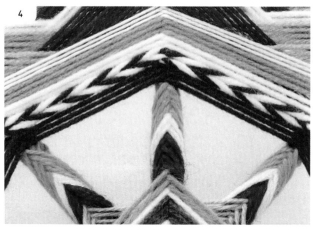

DIAMOND PATTERN

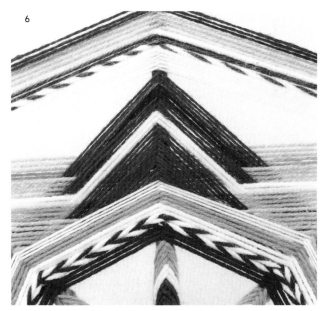

6

9. Begin the diamond pattern (see *Retro Vintage: Diamond Pattern* for detailed instructions) using the top set of sticks, either using the color changing technique or just starting on a new stick. Wrap burgundy yarn around the stick twice and do eight passes in a counter-clockwise direction, then tie off using a simple knot. Next make the teal diamond on the back set of sticks with eight passes of the yarn and tie off. For this mandala I did eight passes of burgundy but only six passes of teal yarn. This is due to variations in the texture and thickness of the yarn and is something I judged by eye. You can also just go by the marking on your dowels to determine where to stop.

10. To make the next diamond, move back to the top set of sticks and do five burgundy passes, then tie off and move to the back set of sticks. Make a color change with the teal yarn and do five passes, always matching the markings on your dowels to ensure you are in the same spot when you stop for each set of sticks.

11. Then tie off and move back to the burgundy yarn on the top set of sticks. Make a color change to white, then make two passes to accent the diamond. Tie off with a simple knot and go back to the teal. Accent the teal with two passes of white yarn and tie off (6).

7

12. Change back to burgundy for the top set of sticks, make four passes, then tie off with a simple knot and move to the back sticks. Make a color change back to teal and do four passes before tying off with another simple knot. Move back to the top set of sticks, this time making a color change to bright purple to do two passes. Color change to soft purple, do one pass as an accent, then color change to burgundy and finish this diamond with three passes. Tie it off with a simple knot.

13. On the back set of sticks, make a color change to green and do three passes. Make a final color change back to teal and do three passes. Tie a simple knot to finish. You have now completed the diamond pattern for this mandala (7).

14. At this point check your dowels are equally spaced. Slight adjustments can be made to each section, and you can also look at the overall symmetry. However if you haven't adjusted your sticks as you went along, don't worry too much if you can't make it perfect. That takes time and practice.

Mindful Moment

Sometimes an adaptable approach is needed. In life nothing is exact or perfect and nor will your yarn be. Sometimes you will need more or fewer passes around the mandala. To adjust for this, have flexibility and go with the flow instead of paddling upstream.

OUTER CIRCLE

15. To finish this mandala we will add a circle pattern (see *Pure and Simple: Circle Pattern* for detailed instructions). Start with a color change to light blue and do five passes round the circle, then color change to white. Do one pass with the white; do not cut the yarn, but add the purple with a clockwise twist. Wrap the initial stick twice to the secure both yarns as if doing a color change, then continue to twist the yarns as you make a pass around the circle to create a slash pattern.

16. Cut the white yarn and continue around the mandala for two more passes with just the dark purple. Switch color and do one complete pass in white, before changing back to teal.

17. Do four passes with the teal yarn, unless you have a lot of space at the end, in which case you may need more. This is a good place to use your judgment – depending on your weaving skill and technique, you may need another pass or two before completing the mandala. When you can see that there is enough space for three burgundy passes, your teal section is done. I only made four passes with teal, then finished with three of burgundy (8). This completes Little Gem – you did a great job!

Star Bright

This is a great mandala to combine several techniques that we've already discussed, with a new embroidery pattern to complete it. These embroidered squares can be arranged into a variety of patterns, so stretch your imagination by playing with them to make your own design, if you feel moved to. For this mandala I've used 14in (35.5cm) dowels to give you a slightly bigger piece to work with.

YOU WILL NEED

Four wooden dowels, 14in (35.5cm) long and ¹⁄₁₆in (2mm) in diameter

Worsted-weight (aran) yarn, 10oz (280g) of each of the following colors: white, dark green, blue, black, orange, yellow, pale purple, green, and burgundy

Essential tools (see *Tools and Materials*)

Finished size: 14 x 14in (35.5 x 35.5cm)

STAR BRIGHT

CENTER

1. Once your sticks are marked and notched (see *Getting Started: Preparing the Dowels*), follow the instructions in *Getting Started: Creating a Double Center* to begin. Take the first two sticks and start by making a total of six wraps in white yarn to form the first center. Make a color change (see *Getting Started: Changing Colors*) to dark green and do two passes, wrapping each stick twice round, then change color again to blue. Do two passes to complete the first center.

2. The second center is made with the other set of sticks. Using dark green, make a total of 12 passes in the square pattern.

3. For this mandala we will use the dagger pattern to hold the two centers together (see *Getting Started: Creating a Double Center – Joining with Daggers*). Start with the 6 o'clock stick and make a color change to black yarn. Make two dagger passes on each of the sticks (1).

DIAMOND PATTERN

4. Change color to the orange yarn and do three passes, working in a diamond pattern on the front set of sticks (see *Retro Vintage: Diamond Pattern*) (2).

5. Now switch to the back set of sticks and do four passes of the yellow yarn in the diamond pattern. My yellow yarn was thinner than the other colors, which is why I made the extra pass. Use your judgment to determine whether you need three or four passes. Next do three passes with dark green yarn on the front sticks, color change to black for three passes on the back sticks, again make three passes on the front sticks in blue, then three passes in pale purple on the back set of sticks (3).

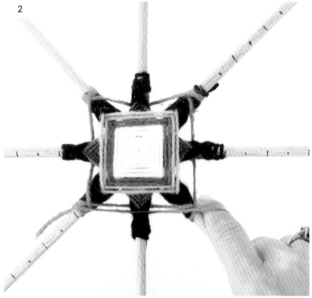

6. Now outline the pattern you have woven with a section of green. Starting with the top set of sticks, color change to green and make five passes, then move to the back set of sticks. Use the color change technique to join the yarns, and do five passes around in green. Tie off. Switch to the top sticks and change to white for two passes. Then tie off and do another two passes of white, this time on the back set of sticks. Finish off with four passes of green yarn on the top sticks, before tying off once more (4).

DAGGERS

7. I wanted to create some negative space for this mandala, so I decided to do daggers here to open up the design before finishing with a circle border. To do this, pick the front set of sticks and make a dagger pattern (see *Insight: Daggers*) in orange yarn for four complete passes on each top set of sticks, tying off between each set.

8. Next move to the back set of sticks and do the dagger pattern, again in orange (5). I finished this mandala with seven full passes on the back sticks for one dagger and five passes for the other (see tip). At this point, make sure you are about the same distance from the end of each stick prior to starting the circle border. If you are off, add another dagger to make it even.

While you're making the daggers it's a good time to check for symmetry. To make the most evenly circular border, I measure and add an extra dagger if necessary to make up for tension issues or weaving corrections. This is also a great time for cleaning up loose ends or trimming extra yarn on the back.

CIRCLE BORDER

9. To start the circle border (see *Pure and Simple: Circle Pattern*) make a color change to dark green and complete three turns. Then do another color change to blue and make three turns before changing back to dark green for two turns.

10. Next make another color change to pale purple and complete two turns, then change to burgundy and do two turns.

11. Finally complete the circle weaving with five turns of blue and two turns of black (6). If you need one more black turn, that is fine.

12. Finish by tying off and tucking or weaving in the yarn end on the reverse of the mandala and glue the stick ends to prevent unraveling (see *General Techniques: Finishing the Mandala*). Let the glue dry completely before starting any embroidery.

EMBROIDERY

13. See *General Techniques: Adding Embroidery.* Thread your tapestry needle with about 18in (46cm) of white yarn for each section of embroidery. Follow the embroidery diagram (7) to stitch the pattern on each of the eight sides of the mandala (8). Always start by bringing your needle up from the back of the mandala, leaving about 1in (2.5cm) of yarn tail to weave neatly into the back of the embroidery to prevent it from unraveling.

14. When you have completed the last square in each embroidered section, flip the mandala over and tuck the loose yarn tails into the embroidered square to finish off that section before beginning the next with a new length of white yarn. When all eight embroidery sections are complete, your mandala is finished. Good job!

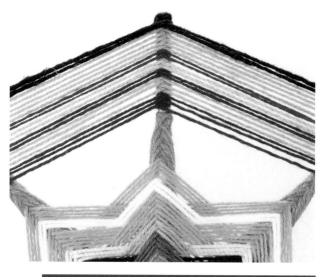

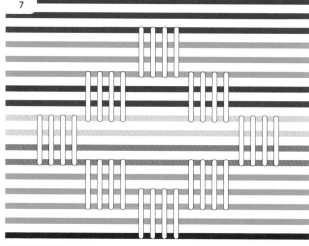

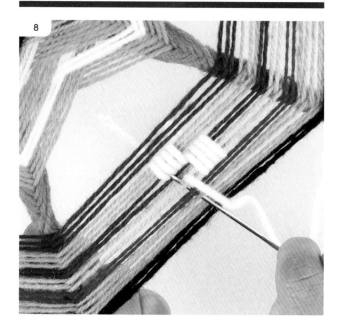

STAR BRIGHT

Sage Brush

This mandala is always a popular one. It is based on an original design by Sami Herbert, but I have switched the colors around to show you how playing with color can help you find new ways to create unusual pieces of art and bring joy. Take a moment to focus on your intention before you begin to weave this mandala - your own choices of color will be influenced by it. And consider involving significant numbers in the design, those that represent special events or are of spiritual importance for you. The number five often represents grace. So let grace carry you....

YOU WILL NEED

Four wooden dowels, 14in (35.5cm) long and 1⁄16in (2mm) in diameter

Worsted-weight (aran) yarn, 6oz (175g) of each of the following colors: white, royal blue, teal, purple, dark brown, orange, camel brown, dark coral, light blue, medium coral, green, and light coral

Essential tools (see *Tools and Materials*)

Finished size: 14 x 14in (35.5 x 35.5cm)

SAGE BRUSH

CENTER

1. Mark and notch your sticks by following the instructions in *Getting Started: Preparing the Dowels*, then take a look at *Getting Started: Creating a Double Center* for how to begin. Start the first center by weaving eight passes in white yarn, then make a color change (see *Getting Started: Changing Colors*) to make two passes of royal blue. Color change again to make three passes of teal, then complete the first center with two passes of white.

2. Next pick up the back sticks and make the second center, making 17 passes of the purple yarn to create a slightly larger center than the front one. Tie off and prepare to attach the two centers together (1).

DIAMOND PATTERN

3. For this mandala we will use the diamond pattern to hold the centers together (see *Getting Started: Creating a Double Center – Joining with the Diamond Pattern*). Take the first center and, starting with the 6 o'clock stick, make a color change to begin with dark brown yarn. Grab the back set of sticks, holding them in your non-dominant hand, and weave the yarn under the back set of sticks and over the top set, as previously described. Make four dark brown passes. Then move to the back set of sticks and do four passes of orange yarn.

4. The next color is camel brown, which is used to outline the central part of the mandala. Make four passes with the top set of sticks, then make a further four passes with the bottom set of sticks. Create a further outline in white by changing to this color and making three passes on the top sticks, then three more passes on the bottom (2).

5. Switch to the top set of sticks and make four passes of the dark coral yarn, then switch to the back sticks and do four in teal. Swap back to the top set of sticks to make four more coral passes, and then make four darker teal green passes on the back sticks. Outline the coral section with two passes of light camel brown yarn, outline the light blue section on the back sticks with one pass of white.

6. This is a nice moment to pause – take time to breathe and realize you have done great work so far. I like to measure at this point to make sure I have finished at approximately the same place on each stick. If you find you haven't, add another pass of either the white or the camel brown outlines to balance the mandala before continuing.

7. When ready, start back with the top set of sticks and do four passes of the medium coral yarn. Then move to the back set of sticks and do four passes with green. When complete, move back to the top set of sticks and do four passes of the light coral yarn and finally move to the back sticks and do the last four passes of the green (3). We are now ready to create the circle border.

CIRCLE BORDER

8. This border is quite wide in order to accommodate the embroidery. See *Pure and Simple: Circle Pattern* for how to weave this simple technique. Begin with four passes in the purple yarn and then make a color change to make four passes in white. Next make three passes in camel brown, then three in medium coral and four in dark coral. At this point you will move to the final wrap of brown. If you have a large area of bare stick to cover you may choose to add more dark coral or just finish up with the brown. I ended with four passes of the dark brown yarn (4).

9. When you are finished, tie off and tuck the yarn tail in on the reverse of the stick and glue your ends to prepare for embroidery (see *General Techniques: Finishing the Mandala*).

Mindful Moment

Why do we make progress in such small steps? I like to think of moving on in the mandala as being like moving in life. It's ok to have a grand vision, but when it's time for movement we need to take one step at a time. This may lead you to a new creation and one that perhaps you did not plan for. Be open to change and follow curiosity – you will have a new design in no time!

EMBROIDERY

10. See *General Techniques: Adding Embroidery*. This embroidery uses the same square that we stitched in the Star Bright mandala. To begin, you will need about 36in (90cm) of royal blue yarn (that's about an arm's length) threaded on your tapestry needle. Insert the needle from the back of the mandala to start, and follow the embroidery diagram (5) to complete the stitching. I like to count four strings for each square, but note that my camel-colored yarn was finer than the other colors so I stitched over five strings in this case (6). You will need to use your judgment to keep your squares "square" (7).

11. Secure your yarn end at the back of the mandala and you're done. Great job!

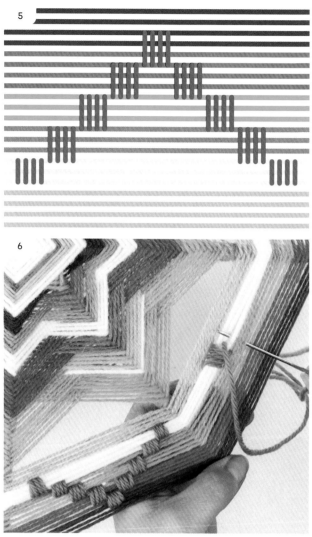

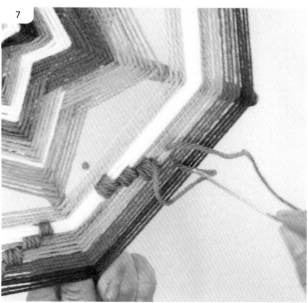

Mindful Moment

When I sit to begin an embroidery I like to return to the word 'intention'. I usually grab my coffee and put on some music that I love to listen to, then I remember my intention for the mandala and begin to draw from the well inside me (see *Getting Started: How to Begin – Setting an Intention*). This is a nice practice as it is a centering technique to help you focus and relax. This will help you with tension and not pulling the squares too tight or making them too loose.

SAGE BRUSH

Golden Way

The final mandala in this section, Golden Way shares a similar design to the two previous mandalas, but this time the colors are inverted for yet another beautiful effect. It combines all the techniques we have used so far: daggers, squares and circles. You'll find there is an almost infinite number of ways to put these patterns together. The color inversion to me reflects how sometimes our life feels turned inside out. Take this idea and invert another pattern to see what magic it can hold for you.

YOU WILL NEED

Four wooden dowels, 12in (30cm) long and ³⁄₁₆in (4mm) in diameter

Worsted-weight (aran) yarn, 6oz (175g) of each of the following colors: white, dark teal, mid teal, light teal, purple, burgundy, orange, yellow, and camel brown

Essential tools (see *Tools and Materials*)

Finished size: 12 x 12in (30 x 30cm)

GOLDEN WAY

CENTER

1. Check *Getting Started: Preparing the Dowels* for instructions on how to mark and notch your sticks, then see *Getting Started: Creating a Double Center* for how to begin. The first center uses two sticks and the white yarn. Begin with six passes of white, then make a color change (see *Getting Started: Changing Colors*) and make one pass of dark teal, then two passes of mid teal, two of light teal, and a final pass of white yarn.

2. Take the other set of sticks to create the second center and make 14 passes with the purple yarn (1).

DAGGERS

3. For this mandala we will use the dagger pattern to hold the centers together (see *Getting Started: Creating a Double Center – Joining with Daggers*). Make four dagger passes in burgundy yarn, then color change to make two orange passes. Next color change again, this time to yellow, and complete two more passes, then make one last color change for two white dagger passes. This completes the daggers for this mandala.

DIAMOND PATTERN

4. For this design I decided to use an alternating diamond technique and began with white. This highlights the daggers and draws the eye to the center. Start on the six o'clock stick and do two passes of white yarn.

5. Switch to the back set of sticks and attach the white yarn with the color change technique before making two passes. Next do two passes in yellow on first the front and then the back sticks, followed by two passes in burgundy on both the front and the back sticks.

6. To frame the center diamond and fill out the middle section of this mandala, start again at the 6 o'clock stick and make three orange passes on the front sticks, then three passes of dark teal on the back sticks. Next make another color change back to orange and do three more passes on the top sticks in the diamond pattern, then switch to the back set of sticks for three passes of mid teal. Highlight this section with one pass of white, starting on the top set of sticks and finishing with the back set of sticks (2).

7. Continue this orange middle section by changing back to the top set of sticks and the orange yarn to do three more passes, then switch back to the mid teal to do three passes on the back set of sticks. Make another three passes of orange on the top sticks, followed by five passes of light teal on the back set of sticks. Move back to the top sticks and finish with about three passes of orange, followed by a similar number in the light teal yarn on the back sticks (3). At this point you can adjust the number of passes to ensure that your final diamond is symmetrical and will allow you to create a nice even circle for the outer border.

CIRCLE BORDER

8. To complete the weaving of this mandala, start with five passes in white yarn in a circle pattern (see *Pure and Simple: Circle Pattern*), then color change to make two passes in yellow.

9. At this point use your judgment to decide how many passes are required in the remaining two colors. I did two passes in camel brown, and completed with three passes in burgundy. Tie off and tuck the yarn tail in on the reverse of the mandala, then glue your ends to prevent unraveling (see *General Techniques: Finishing the Mandala*).

EMBROIDERY

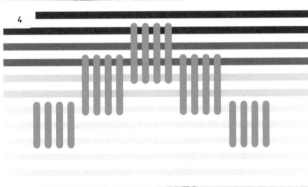

10. See *General Techniques: Adding Embroidery*. The embroidery for this mandala uses the same squares pattern that we have used before. I like to use four stitches to make each square, stepping them up and down the circle border to make the pattern. With a length of mid teal yarn in your needle, follow the diagram (4) and take a close look at the photo (5) to complete the five squares in each section of embroidery.

11. Stitch this pattern eight times around the circle border. Secure all your ends and prepare to hang up your mandala (see *General Techniques: Finishing the Mandala*). You are done!

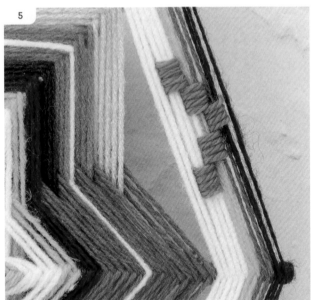

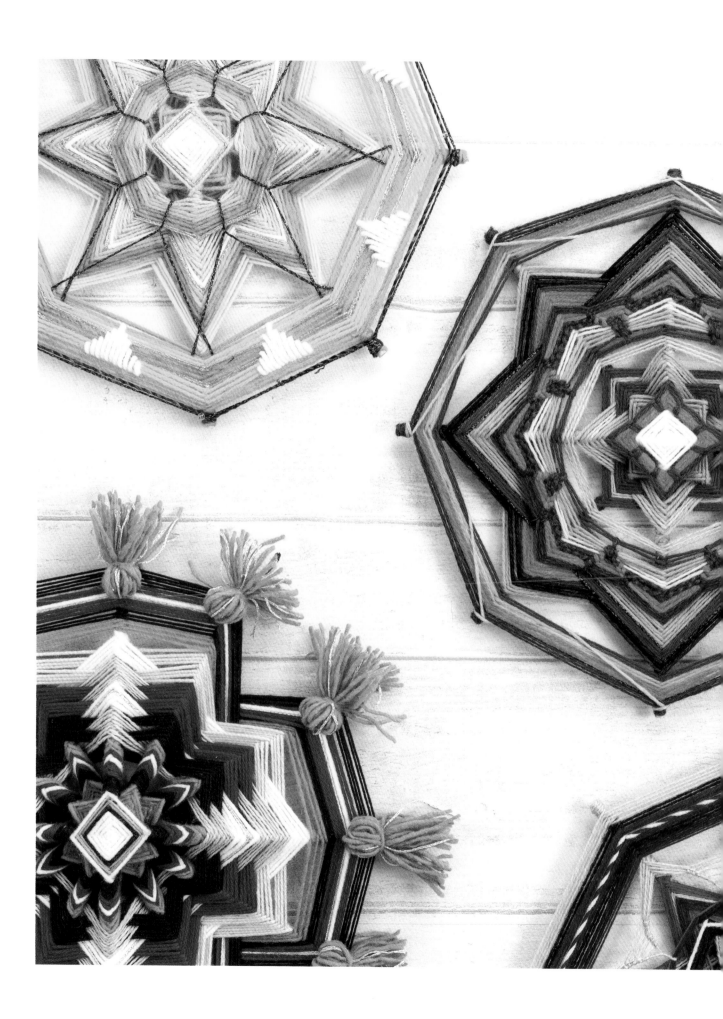

Energy Center Mandalas

Energy centers are the spinning wheels of vibratory energy in our human body. Linked to the major centers of our wellbeing, they work to regulate our immune system, organ function and emotions. Although this section covers just a few of the energy centers in our bodies, these are considered the major ones. I have given an overview of each center for your weaving meditation and to help you set an intention (see *Getting Started: How to Begin – Setting an Intention*) before you begin.

Root

The root is the center of our connection to our community and to those we interact with. It reflects our ability to create and sustain the resources we need for our human survival. This center's function is like the root of a tree: if it is weak, the tree is weak; if it is vibrant, strong and supported, the tree is too. An intention for this mandala could be something like: I am continually receiving all that I need and more to create and sustain vibrant physical health, relationships and my environment.

YOU WILL NEED

Four wooden dowels, 12in (30cm) long and ³⁄₁₆in (4mm) in diameter

Worsted-weight (aran) yarn, 6oz (175g) of each of the following colors: white, bright red, dark red, taupe, dark brown, burgundy, and mid red

Essential tools (see *Tools and Materials*)

Finished size: 12 x 12in (30 x 30cm)

ROOT

A FIRST CENTER

See *Getting Started: Preparing the Dowels, Creating a Double Center* and *Changing Colors*

Make the first center with six passes of white, one of bright red, then add white and do a twist pattern for one pass (see *Little Gem: Circle Pattern with Herringbone*, but only make one pass round the sticks). Finish this center with one pass in bright red.

B SECOND CENTER

For the second center, make 11 passes in bright red yarn.

C DIAMOND PATTERN

See *Getting Started: Creating a Double Center – Joining with the Diamond Pattern*

To attach the two centers, make three passes in dark red on the front sticks and three passes in dark red on the back sticks.

D STAR PATTERN

This is a new pattern that we have not tried yet. It creates space with more of a triangle effect, made by the points of the star.

1. Start with the 6 o'clock stick and make a color change to taupe yarn. Once you have wrapped your stick twice, go behind two sticks to the third stick to the right and wrap twice.

2. Next, go under the next two sticks again to the third stick in a counter-clockwise direction. Repeating this pattern will create the star shape. Do this four times to complete the star.

E HEXAGON PATTERN

This is another new pattern, which I have highlighted with a white outline.

1. To start this section, begin with the 6 o'clock stick and make three dagger passes using just the 6 o'clock and 12 o'clock sticks in white yarn (see *Insight: Daggers*).

2. Select the stick directly to the right of the 6 o'clock stick, color change to dark brown and make one pass on the first three sticks only.

3. Go under the 12 o'clock stick, and continue this pass, wrapping the opposite set of three sticks.

4. Wrap the yarn back under the 6 o'clock stick, then repeat the pattern three more times. Make a color change and highlight the hexagon with one pass of white.

F CIRCLE PATTERN

Remember this pattern is simply wrapping from stick to stick (see *Pure and Simple: Circle Pattern*). Make three passes in burgundy, three passes in dark red and one pass in bright red.

G LARGE STAR

Referring to the Star Pattern instructions above, make three passes in bright red, three passes in burgundy, and one pass in dark red to give a slight outline. Make two passes in taupe, one pass in bright red, and three of mid red to finish this star pattern.

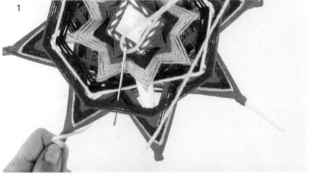

H FLOWER PATTERN

We are now going to do a knot pattern based on the circle technique to create a fan-like flower design. This is another new technique.

1. Start by making a color change to taupe yarn, and wrap twice around the 6 o'clock stick. Then wrap your yarn over the top of the circle (F), passing under it (1) and coming up between the taupe string and the large star pattern (2). This creates a half knot.

2. Wrap round the next stick to create the first flower knot. Repeat this action until you have come back to the beginning. Finish by wrapping twice around the first stick.

3. Next thread the yarn through about 1in (2.5cm) above the knot you just made (3). Pull the yarn tight. Now take the yarn to the right of the first flower knot you made and loop it round in the same way on the other side of this knot (4). Pull the string tight to complete the second part of the 'flower petal' (5).

4. Repeat this step around the rest of the sticks until you have completed five circuits of the flower pattern. Note the beautiful 'v' shape the yarn makes on the sticks, and the strings drawn to the middle section to make the petals of the flower design.

I OUTER CIRCLE

Use the mid red to make two passes, then make two passes of burgundy. Make two more passes with dark brown, followed by two passes in bright red. Twist in some white yarn to make one complete pass of the circle (see *Little Gem: Circle Pattern with Herringbone* for how to add the white yarn). Return to the mid red for two passes, then use dark brown for two passes. Add four to five passes of taupe and finish the mandala in the usual way (see *General Techniques: Finishing the Mandala*).

Vitality

This energy center is necessary for spiritual growth. Vitality is not limited to age or gender, but provides essential support for intelligence, wisdom and creativity. Its purpose is to move the creative life fires from deep in the body to the higher centers. This process increases consciousness and our ability to manifest what we truly long for. An intention for this mandala may be: my vitality center is an ever-renewing fount of life-force, inspiring all my energy centers, nourishing and materializing my deepest longings.

YOU WILL NEED

Four wooden dowels, 14in (35.5cm) long and ⅟₁₆in (2mm) in diameter

Worsted-weight (aran) yarn, 8oz (225g) of each of the following colors: white, bright yellow, taupe, golden yellow, bright orange, medium orange, and dark red-orange

Essential tools (see *Tools and Materials*)

Finished size: 14 x 14in (35.5 x 35.5cm)

VITALITY

A FIRST CENTER

See *Getting Started: Preparing the Dowels, Creating a Double Center* and *Changing Colors*

To begin, make six passes of white yarn, two passes of bright yellow, two passes of taupe and one pass in golden yellow.

B SECOND CENTER

For the second center make 13 passes in white yarn.

C DIAMOND PATTERN

See *Getting Started: Creating a Double Center – Joining with the Diamond Pattern*

To attach the two centers, make three passes in the diamond pattern on the front sticks in bright orange, then switch to the back sticks and do four passes in medium orange. Go back to the top set of sticks and make four passes of dark red-orange, then move to the bottom sticks and do four passes with bright orange.

D CIRCLE PATTERN

See *Pure and Simple: Circle Pattern*

Color change to taupe and make three circle passes. Change to bright orange for three passes, then to medium orange for three passes and dark red-orange for three more passes.

E ARROW DESIGN

Before you start this new technique, take a length of yarn of about 3ft (90cm) in each of these colors: bright yellow, bright orange and dark red-orange.

1. Attach the yellow yarn to the six o'clock stick using the color change method. Insert the yellow yarn over and around the circle, threading it back over itself. Make sure this loop is at the midpoint between the sticks (1).

2. Take the yarn counter-clockwise and wrap it around the next stick (2). Repeat a total of eight times, between each set of sticks.

3. Repeat steps 1 and 2 with the bright orange yarn, but instead of looping the yarn over the inner edge of the circle, thread it between the taupe and bright orange strings of the circle, making the orange 'dash' to the left of the yellow one as shown (3).

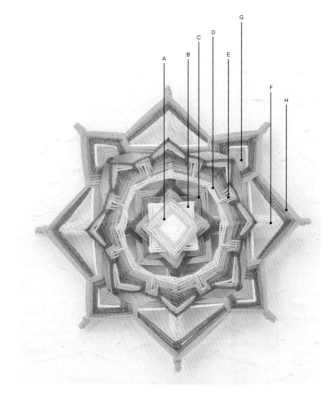

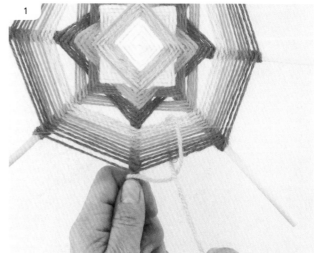

4. Next, make another dash to the right of the yellow one, using the same method. Do this for the remainder of the circle, making a dash on each side of the yellow.

5. Repeat to make another orange dash either side of the ones you have already made, this time making them shorter by threading the yarn through between the middle and last bright orange string of the circle. Repeat to add a pair of dark red-orange dashes each side of the arrow pattern, this time threading the yarn between the bright orange and dark red-orange strings of the circle. Make a second pair of dashes either side of the arrow in dark-red orange, bringing the yarn through between the second and third dark red-orange strings of the circle (4).

F DAGGERS

See *Insight: Daggers*

Make five bright yellow and four taupe dagger passes on each stick.

G SQUARE PATTERN

See *Insight: Square Pattern*

Make four passes in a square pattern in bright orange yarn, going under the dagger, and only wrapping round two pairs of the sticks. Next make five medium orange passes, followed by one in white yarn.

H ARROW WAVE

Use the knot method for the Arrow Design (see above), but make a wave shape, building on the knot as you go.

1. On the top set of sticks, secure the dark orange-red yarn to the 6 o'clock stick. Move in a counter-clockwise direction, wrapping the yarn over the square pattern towards the middle, then bring it up through to make a knot before wrapping it twice round the next stick (in the back set of sticks). Make sure your knot is closer to this stick than the one you started from (see main photo).

2. Do the same thing to the right of the next stick (again see main photo). Then wrap the yarn around the 3 o'clock stick twice. This makes the arrow wave.

3. Repeat, making two more dark orange-red passes, two mid orange passes and three bright orange passes. Then finish the mandala in the usual way (see *General Techniques: Finishing the Mandala*).

Solar

The solar energy center is the gathering place of the sun, a place where your personal will resides. Personal power, self-confidence, and the ability to persevere to achieve what you truly long for all come from the solar center. This is where our emotional maturity springs from. If you struggle in this area, an intention for this mandala may be something like this: I matter, I am valuable, strong and confident. My emotions are balanced and serve my greatest good.

YOU WILL NEED

Four wooden dowels, 12in (30cm) long and ³⁄₁₆in (4mm) in diameter

Worsted-weight (aran) yarn, 6oz (175g) of each of the following colors: white, pale taupe, taupe, bright yellow, golden yellow, sparkle yellow, mid yellow, golden darker yellow and metallic gold, and black

Essential tools (see *Tools and Materials*)

Finished size: 12 x 12in (30 x 30cm)

SOLAR

A FIRST CENTER

See *Getting Started: Preparing the Dowels, Creating a Double Center* and *Changing Colors*

Make six passes in white, change to pale taupe for one pass, then taupe for a final pass.

B SECOND CENTER

Use bright yellow to make 11 passes.

C JOINING CIRCLE

See *Pure and Simple: Circle Pattern*

Using a circle technique is the trickiest way of joining the centers together. I recommend you clear a flat surface such as your kitchen table to lay your mandala flat while you work until you have perfected this method.

1. Start at the 6 o'clock position and wrap the stick twice to secure the taupe yarn. Moving counter-clockwise for one complete pass, wrap the yarn twice round each stick as you would with a regular circle. Do not pull each stick too tightly and check that there is equal tension throughout the first wrap.

2. Make a second pass in taupe yarn around the circle, then change colors and do three bright yellow, three golden yellow and two sparkle yellow passes. The two centers should now be firmly attached.

D STAR PATTERN

See *Root: Star Pattern*

Start with the taupe yarn and make six passes, then one pass of white to outline the star and two of yellow sparkle yarn. Make another color change and add two passes in bright yellow, then three in golden yellow. Finish the star with four passes of mid yellow.

E CIRCLE BORDER

Start this simple circle pattern with three passes of golden yellow. Then, with color changes between each, complete the following: two passes in bright yellow, two passes in sparkle yellow, two passes of dark yellow, two more passes in sparkle yellow, three passes in bright yellow, two passes in golden darker yellow and a final pass in metallic gold and black. Glue the ends of your sticks to prevent unraveling and leave them to dry (see *General Techniques: Finishing the Mandala*).

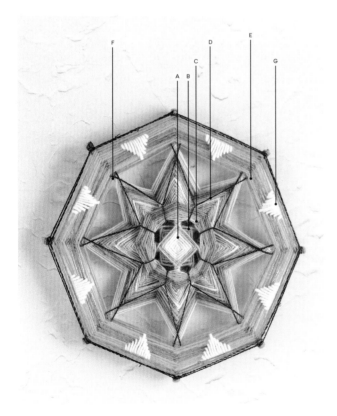

This mandala has the sweet addition of metallic thread. I highly recommend using this, especially for festive decorations. Use it in small amounts for added pizzazz.

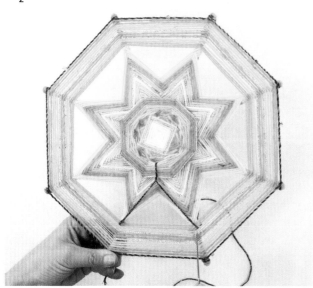

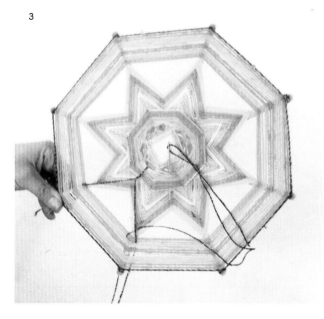

F KNOTTING PATTERN

Thread about 44in (112cm) of metallic gold and black yarn in your needle. I use two arm lengths!

1. Thread the needle through from the back of the mandala to the left of your first stick, between the golden yellow and bright yellow strings of the outer circle. Then insert your needle into the center of the joining circle and bring it out under the golden yarn of this circle and over the star pattern (1), making sure it passes to the left of the yarn going into the circle so that it catches it to make a loop.

2. Take the yarn over towards the next stick (directly to the right of your start point) and insert your needle back through between the golden and bright yellow strings of the outer circle, to the right of the stick (2).

3. Make the next knot by bringing the needle up to the left of the stick just as before, taking the yarn into the joining circle, over the star and back through the outer circle (3). Repeat the pattern till you have gone all the way around the mandala. Glue the stick ends ready for embroidery (see *General Techniques: Finishing the Mandala*).

G EMBROIDERY

See *Earth and Fire: Triangle Embroidery* and *General Techniques: Adding Embroidery*

Start by inserting the white yarn between the gold and yellow strings of the outer circle. Make each stitch two strings longer than the previous one, until you have made six stitches, then step them back down in size to create the triangle. Complete this embroidery on each side of the mandala, a total of eight times (see main photo).

Heart

This center radiates love, forgiveness, compassion, and the ability to spontaneously heal. A healthy and balanced heart center allows you to care for yourself with loving kindness and strength, while also being a powerful source of wellbeing for others. The ability to give yourself in service is necessary for true prosperity. The love that flows from this center connects to the heart of universal energy. An intention for this mandala could be: compassion and forgiveness radiate from my heart. I love sharing my gifts. Prosperity flows to me in this state.

YOU WILL NEED

Four wooden dowels, 12in (30cm) long and ³⁄₁₆in (4mm) in diameter

Worsted-weight (aran) yarn, 2oz (55g) of white and bronze/gold sparkle, and 6oz (175g) of each of the following colors: bright green, dark green, light green, yellow, olive green, and very dark purple

Essential tools (see *Tools and Materials*)

Finished size: 12 x 12in (30 x 30cm)

HEART

A FIRST CENTER

See Getting Started: Preparing the Dowels, Creating a Double Center, and Changing Colors

Begin the center with six passes of white yarn, then three passes of bright green. To form the slashes in the middle we will use a knot technique.

1. Thread about 36in (91cm) of dark green yarn on your needle. Secure the yarn end to the 6 o'clock stick, then insert the needle between the white and the bright green strings from the front, bringing the needle round under the center to the front and catching the yarn to make the first slash (1).

2. Repeat to make another slash on the same side, then take the yarn to the next stick and wrap twice. Work round the center, making two slashes on each side (2).

3. Make another pass round the center, making slashes as before (3).

B SECOND CENTER

Make 11 passes with light green to complete the second center.

C DIAMOND PATTERN

See Getting Started: Creating a Double Center – Joining with the Diamond Pattern

To attach the two centers, make three diamond pattern passes in light green on the front sticks, then four passes in dark green on the back sticks. Make two yellow and two light green passes on the front sticks. Switch to the back sticks and do two yellow passes followed by three dark green passes.

D INNER CIRCLE

See Pure and Simple: Circle Pattern

Start with three yellow circle passes followed by three dark green passes, then three light green passes followed by two white passes. This completes the circle.

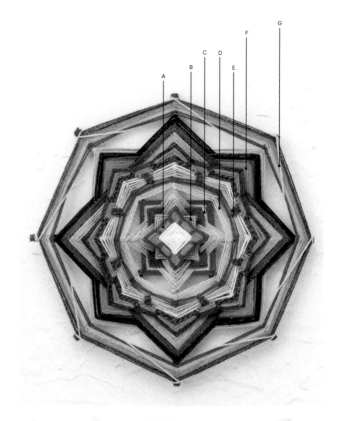

1

2

3

E ARROW DESIGN

See *Vitality: Arrow Design*

Secure the dark green yarn to your starting stick, and insert your needle through between the yellow and dark green strings of the inner circle. Come up behind the circle, make the knot and move to the next stick, wrapping twice. Continue the pattern around the entire mandala. For the second pass make the slashes to both left and right of the first slash, this time going between the second and third dark green strings. Change color to bright green. Make another pass around the circle, making knots. Make a short slash to the left and right of the dark green ones, going between the two white strings. Then do another pass, this time going between the white and dark green. Finish with a color change to dark green and make two more passes, inserting the yarn between the dark green strings on the first pass and between the two dark green strings on the second. Make knots to create short slashes to the left and right of each of the arrow elements (4).

F DIAMOND PATTERN

See *Retro Vintage: Diamond Pattern*

Secure the light green yarn using the color change technique and, on the front sticks, do five passes in the diamond pattern, followed by one pass of bronze or gold sparkle yarn. Then do three passes in dark green followed by one more in the sparkle yarn. Switch to the back set of sticks and make four passes of bright green, followed by two passes of olive green, and then three passes of very dark purple. Swap back to the front sticks and make three very dark purple passes. Repeat the three purple passes on the front sticks then move once again to the back sticks and finish with three passes of the light green.

G OUTER CIRCLE WITH TWIST

Begin the last circle with a color change and make two passes in olive green yarn, then two in light green. Follow that with two bright green passes and one bronze or gold sparkle yarn, and then three dark green passes to finish.

To make the twist pattern (see main photo), secure the yellow yarn on one stick. Wrap it under the mandala and come out inside the outer circle, then take the yarn over the top and wrap around the next stick to secure it. Then go under the circle again and bring the yarn round and out to the next stick. Repeat this pattern all the way round, and finish the mandala in the usual way (see *General Techniques: Finishing the Mandala*).

4

Throat

This center links the creative fire of the vitality center with the infinite creative force of divine self. Purity of expression with our words can align us with universal truths. It links the heart and the mind in a way that can create expressions of love, purity, truth, and beauty. What do you think you will create and express? An intention for this mandala may be this: I direct all my expressions to be in alignment with universal truths. I use the power of my voice in service to the compassionate awakening of my whole self and of the world.

YOU WILL NEED

Four wooden dowels, 12in (30cm) long and ³⁄₁₆in (4mm) in diameter

Worsted-weight (aran) yarn, 6oz (175g) of each of the following colors: white, dark blue, medium blue, taupe, seafoam green, teal, metallic silver, and purple

Essential tools (see *Tools and Materials*)

Finished size: 12 x 12in (30 x 30cm)

THROAT

A CENTERS

See *Getting Started: Preparing the Dowels, Creating a Double Center* and *Changing Colors*

For the first center, make five white passes, one dark blue pass, two in medium blue, one in taupe and then two dark blue passes.

For the smaller, second center make seven passes in seafoam green. Note that this center is behind the first, and because it is smaller it does not show from the front.

B DAGGERS

See *Getting Started: Creating a Double Center – Joining with Daggers*

Change color to dark blue and make four daggers on the top set of sticks. On the bottom set of sticks, make four seafoam green daggers.

C DIAMOND PATTERN

See *Retro Vintage: Diamond Pattern*

On the top set of sticks, make two diamond passes of dark blue. Switch to the bottom set of sticks and make two passes of seafoam green. Move back to the top sticks and make three passes with dark blue yarn, and then swap to the back sticks to make three passes with seafoam green. On the top set of sticks make three medium blue passes, then on the back sticks make three passes in teal. Return to the top set of sticks and make one pass of white. Finally make two passes of metallic silver on the bottom set of sticks.

D INNER CIRCLE

See *Pure and Simple: Circle Pattern*

Create the inner circle by making two passes in dark blue and one in metallic silver yarn.

E STAR PATTERN

See *Root: Star Pattern*

Make five passes in teal blue yarn, one pass of white and one pass of metallic silver, followed by three passes of seafoam green. Next make two passes in dark blue yarn.

F CIRCLE AND ARROW
WAVE PATTERN

See *Vitality: Arrow Design* and *Arrow Wave*

In a circle pattern, make three dark blue and three purple passes, then three seafoam green and four teal passes. Now you are ready to create the wave pattern.

Make a color change to dark blue on your first stick and insert the yarn between the first and second dark blue string of the circle. Make a knot as described in *Vitality: Arrow Wave*, then move to the next stick. Do this around the entire mandala, then repeat the same pattern again, inserting the yarn in the same spot. You will now have two 'dashes'. For the next dash, insert the yarn between the purple and dark blue circle strings and repeat this knot around the mandala. Next, insert your yarn between the two purple circle strings and work again around the mandala. You have now completed four dashes. For the final dark blue pass, insert the yarn one string below the last dash between the fifth and sixth strings from the center of the circle, just short of the last purple string. Make the knot and again repeat all around the mandala. Highlight the arrow wave with purple, inserting the yarn between the purple and seafoam green circle strings and making a final round of knots.

G OUTER DIAMOND PATTERN

Starting on the top set of sticks, make six passes of teal and four of seafoam green in the diamond pattern. Switch to the bottom sticks and make six teal passes followed by four passes of seafoam green. This can vary depending on your weaving technique, so remember that it is ok to increase or reduce the number of passes if needed. Finish the mandala in the usual way (see *General Techniques: Finishing the Mandala*).

Note that this mandala differs from all the other double center designs in this book, in that the second center is smaller than the one at the front, so it cannot be seen. It gives depth nevertheless and adds dimension to the design.

Eyebrow

This is the center of the higher self, where the motivating force of higher consciousness, our free will, resides. It is necessary for true understanding – the ability to synthesize facts and experiences in relationship to deeper values and universal patterns. An intention for this mandala may look like this: I am capable of true understanding, I naturally process the thoughts and events of my life. I am in alignment with divine purpose. I flow with the infinite abundance of the universe and easily manifest my purest heart's wishes.

YOU WILL NEED

Four wooden dowels, 12in (30cm) long and ³⁄₁₆in (4mm) in diameter

Worsted-weight (aran) yarn, 6oz (175g) of each of the following colors: white, gray, deep blue, indigo, mid blue, purple, metallic silver, and off-white

Essential tools (see *Tools and Materials*)

Finished size: 12 x 12in (30 x 30cm)

EYEBROW

A FIRST CENTER

See Getting Started: Preparing the Dowels, Creating a Double Center and Changing Colors

Start with eight passes in white yarn, followed by two in gray, one in blue-black, two in deep blue, three in indigo, and one in gray yarn. Note that my gray yarn is very fine and thin. You may choose a thicker yarn – just pay attention to the results and make adjustments. You want this center to be about 2¾ x 2¾in (7 x 7cm).

B SECOND CENTER

For the second center, I made 16 passes of mid blue. You want this center to be slightly bigger than the first one, so just use the yarn you have then adjust the size accordingly with more or fewer passes.

C DIAMOND PATTERN

See Getting Started: Creating a Double Center – Joining with the Diamond Pattern

To attach the two centers, start with the top set of sticks and make four passes in deep blue using the diamond pattern. Then make four passes on the back set of sticks using a blue-black yarn.

D CIRCLE PATTERN WITH HERRINGBONE

See Little Gem: Circle Pattern with Herringbone

Make a circle pass in white yarn, then twist the gray yarn with the white and continue round the circle. Reverse the twist for one pass round the circle to complete the herringbone pattern.

E DIAMOND PATTERN

See *Retro Vintage: Diamond Pattern*

Start on the front sticks with five passes of purple, then two of mid blue and two of gray. Switch to the back set of sticks and do eight deep blue passes, two gray and four blue-black passes.

F FIRST DAGGERS

See *Insight: Daggers*

Change to white yarn and make two white, three off-white and two metallic silver dagger passes on the top set of sticks only.

G HEXAGON PATTERN

See *Root: Hexagon Pattern*

Make a color change and begin with two passes in white yarn. These will go under the 6 o'clock and the 12 o'clock sticks only. Next twist in the metallic silver yarn with the white and make one hexagon pass around the mandala. Then make two blue-black passes before twisting in the mid blue yarn for one pass, then reversing the twist for one pass to complete the herringbone pattern. Add two more passes with blue-black yarn to finish the hexagon.

H SECOND DAGGERS

Start with four purple dagger passes on just the 6 o'clock and 12 o'clock sticks. Then on the remaining top sticks (the 3 o'clock and 9 o'clock sticks), make two purple passes. Switch back to the 6 and 12 o'clock sticks and make three off-white and two metallic silver dagger passes. Swap back to the 3 and 9 o'clock sticks and make three off-white and two metallic silver daggers. Finally, add two white daggers to the 6 and 12 o'clock sticks. More can be added here if needed – just make sure all your sticks have 1in (2.5cm) of space left for the border circle.

I BORDER CIRCLE AND KNOTTING DESIGN

See *Vitality: Arrow Design*

Create the outer circle with five passes of mid blue, then two passes of the metallic silver yarn. Next do three passes of the purple yarn and two passes of blue-black color, then three passes of the purple again. For the final design element we will use the knot pattern like the arrow design in the Vitality mandala. Make a color change to metallic silver and bring the yarn round the outer circle strings forming a knot, then secure the yarn to the next stick. Do this all the way around the mandala, making three passes in total to complete the knotting design. Finish the mandala in the usual way (see *General Techniques: Finishing the Mandala*).

Crown

This center opens us up to receive the highest love and light of the universe, pouring it through every part of our being to support our highest and healthiest healing. It grows as we develop the lower energy centers, then flows out to all humanity, even as we nurture it for ourselves. An intention for this mandala might be: I intuitively know what is needed in every moment, I am fully aligned with divine will. I embody gratitude, compassion and love for myself, and this freely flows to all humanity.

YOU WILL NEED

Six wooden dowels, 12in (30cm) long and ³⁄₁₆in (4mm) in diameter

Worsted-weight (aran) yarn, 6oz (175g) of each of the following colors: white, dark purple, light blue, gold, gray, vibrant purple, pale pink, and metallic silver

Essential tools (see *Tools and Materials*)

Finished size: 12 x 12in (30 x 30cm)

CROWN

A FIRST CENTER

See *General Techniques: A Note on Twelve-sided Mandalas; Getting Started: Preparing the Dowels, Creating the First Center* and *Changing Colors*

Note that this is a twelve-sided mandala and therefore has three centers. Start the first center by making six passes with white yarn, then one dark purple and two in light blue. Highlight this center with one pass of white.

B SECOND AND THIRD CENTERS

Take another pair of sticks and make 12 passes of gold yarn for the second center. Repeat to make the third center. It is more critical in a twelve-sided mandala that the back two centers are slightly bigger than the first, so be sure to pay careful attention to this.

C JOINING DAGGERS

See *Getting Started: Creating a Double Center – Joining with Daggers*

1. Place the three four-sided crosses on top of one another to get an idea of the distance needed between the sticks. For this design we want the sticks equidistant from one another, but you may find it easier at this point to hold the two lower pieces together as if you were starting an eight-sided mandala but with an extra set of sticks. Begin to join the first and second centers by working a dagger pattern in dark purple yarn. After the first dagger, the two sets of sticks will be loosely held together (1). Make three dark purple dagger wraps.

2. Now, attach the third set of sticks and create the second dark purple dagger, starting on the second stick of the top set of sticks. Hold the three crosses together with your left hand and wrap with your right as you move the yarn under the dowels to secure them together (2). This set of daggers secures the third center, as you can see from the back (3). Make three dark purple dagger wraps. At this point, if you had the two bottom crosses stacked together you can fan them out so that all the arms lie equidistant from one another.

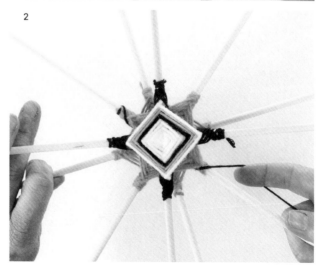

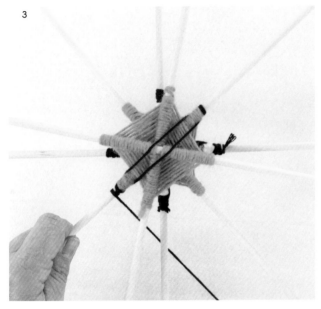

3

D DAGGERS

See *Insight: Daggers*

On each stick make two dagger wraps with the vibrant purple yarn and one wrap with white, finishing with two wraps of gold. Do a simple knot to tie off.

E DIAMOND PATTERN

See *Retro Vintage: Diamond Pattern*

Start with the 6 o'clock stick and make three passes in a diamond pattern in gray yarn, wrapping round each of the sticks in the top set, and going under the sticks in between (4).

F CROSS PATTERN

1. To begin the cross, secure the dark purple yarn to the stick to the left of the 6 o'clock stick. Take the yarn under the 6 o'clock stick, wrap it twice around the next stick, then go under the next three sticks (5).

4

5

CROWN

2. Wrap the yarn twice round the next stick, then go under the 12 o'clock stick, wrap twice round the next stick, then go under the next three sticks to return to the starting point (6). Repeat this process to make a total of four passes with the dark purple yarn.

3. Work this pattern again, starting on the stick to the left of the 3 o'clock stick. When you have completed four passes in dark purple you will have created the cross.

You will now alternate the diamond and cross patterns for this section of the design. Remember to make both parts of the cross pattern each time. Make another diamond with four passes of the gray yarn. Make a cross with four passes of the dark purple yarn. Make the next diamond with two white passes, two metallic silver passes and one white pass. Make the next cross with four passes of the vibrant purple yarn. Make another diamond with four gray passes. Make another cross with four passes of vibrant purple yarn. Make a diamond with four passes of gray yarn, then a cross with four passes of pale pink, followed by a diamond of four passes of white yarn and one more cross made with four passes of pale pink.

G CROSS PATTERN VARIATION

You will now make a variation on the cross pattern, using different sticks. For the first part of the cross, use the 6 and 12 o'clock sticks in the top set of sticks, plus the ones to the right and left as a set. Work this part of the cross as you did the previous cross – but this time, instead off passing the yarn under the 6 and 12 o'clock sticks, wrap the yarn around them twice. Make three passes in the gold yarn.

Make three dark purple passes, then three vibrant purple ones, then one silver and one white pass, then two vibrant purple passes, followed by six dark purple passes. Change to the other set of sticks – the 9 and 3 o'clock set – and do one silver, one white, and two purple passes.

Now complete the other part of the cross by repeating the same colors and number of passes on the 3 and 9 o'clock sticks and the sticks either side of them (7).

Mindful Moment

In life, attention to detail and observing ourselves in the moment is true presence. Focusing on the details of life can become less of a chore and more of a delight. This practice has helped me find my inner presence in all of my doings and can become a joy for you as well.

H TASSELS

See *Blue Horizon: Integrated Tassels*

To make the tassels, use about 20 strings, mostly of gold yarn with about five strands of metallic silver. Follow the instructions for Integrated Tassels in the Blue Horizon mandala, and when tying the tassels to the Crown mandala thread one string to the right of the stick between the vibrant purple and dark purple, and the other string to the left of the stick at the same spot. Bring the tassel-tying string back up through the bottom of the mandala between the second and third strings and then back through the first and second strings before tying off at the back. I trimmed the tassels to be around 1½in (4cm). Finish the mandala in the usual way (see *General Techniques: Finishing the Mandala*).

General Techniques

As well as the all-important instructions on how to finish off your mandala and hang it for display, this section contains some of my best advice for avoiding frustration and creating a professional-looking mandala.

GETTING THE BEST RESULTS

Making mandalas is all about balance and centering, mentally and physically. It's important to stay focused on all elements of the mandala – the colors, the evenness, the spacing, and so on – throughout the process to ensure you create a professional-looking mandala.

TENSION AND DOWEL SPACING

It is important to manage the tension of your yarn as you make each wrap. Not too tight, not too loose. I have talked in detail about tension in the Getting Started section at the beginning of this book. I recommend measuring the spacing between the end of each of your dowels after every color change, and making adjustments as needed. Don't be afraid to unwind and start over.

A NOTE ON 12-SIDED MANDALAS

It is significantly more challenging to keep the three centers together in a twelve-sided mandala than the two centers for an eight-sided mandala. The sticks are often loose and are able move from side to side until your yarn is wrapped about quarter of the way up them. It is even more important to manage the distance between the sticks to ensure that they are equidistant at every phase. Keep in mind that different design elements will provide more stability than others – which can be helpful or make things more difficult. For instance, securing the centers with daggers is considerably less stable than if you join them with a diamond pattern. Additionally, the circle pattern locks the distance between the arms, so if you decide to use a circle early in the design it is critically important to ensure that the sticks are evenly spaced at that point. Also bear in mind that adjustments made to the distance between the sticks later on will affect the tension of the yarn closer to the center. For that reason, try to secure the even spacing between the sticks early on, and avoid making large adjustments later.

The construction of a twelve-sided mandala gives it a depth, which also makes the alignment more critical to keep track of than in an eight-sided mandala. This added dimension means there is a difference between how the yarn is angled in the design elements that are on the bottom-most set of sticks compared to those on the top. Therefore, be sure to watch your notches very closely to ensure that your designs are even on each stick. This will require a little more adjusting of how many wraps you do on each arm – a design element you only wrapped once on the topmost sticks may take two wraps on the middle ones and sometimes even three wraps on the bottom.

Just as the rear center in an eight-sided mandala should be larger than the front one, so the third center of a twelve-sided mandala should be larger still. My rule of thumb that the third center should be three wraps larger than the first.

COMMON DESIGN ELEMENTS

The options for design are limited only by your creativity. I've tried here to give you a starting place for making the patterns that I commonly use as foundations for my mandalas. I recommend that you also look at other pieces to gather inspiration.

1. DAGGERS

This element creates negative space within the mandala and allows you to add small pops of color. It is also one of the techniques I recommend for attaching the sets of sticks together if you have more than one center. To find out how to make daggers, see *Insight: Daggers*.

2. CIRCLE

This simple pattern wraps the yarn round each of the sticks around the whole mandala. When creating a circle pattern, ensure that you are using the guide marks on your dowels to check that you have each wrap at about the same distance from the center on each dowel. This will ensure that your circle is not lop-sided. For instructions on this technique, see *Pure and Simple: Circle Pattern*.

3. DIAMOND

As well as being another way to secure multiple centers together, this pattern frames the mandala and is recommended as you move toward the outer edge of your design. See *Retro Vintage: Diamond Pattern* for detailed instructions on this technique.

4. STAR

This shape adds sharp corners like the tips of a star. It also can fill in any negative space from the back with a color. You can wrap every third arm on an eight-sided mandala or every fifth arm on a twelve-sided mandala for a regular star, but other shapes are possible too. See *Root: Star Pattern* to find out how to make this pattern.

The more sets of sticks you have, the more shapes become available, such as the 'cross' in the Crown mandala. Experiment with skipping different numbers of sticks when wrapping. Play around with this to see what shapes you can come up with!

FINISHING THE MANDALA

* As you move toward the perimeter of your mandala, pay close attention to having each wrap on each dowel at the same distance from the edge. You may have to compensate with one more or one less wrap to make them even. Paying attention to this from the beginning will help minimize the need to make significant adjustments at the end.

* Once you get to about two or three wraps from the edge, as you change to the last color, leave a long tail of yarn sticking out on the bottom dowel instead of covering it with the next yarn wrap. This will give you something to tie your last wrap of yarn to. Once you have made your way to the end of the dowel, cut the yarn leaving a tail of about 2in (5cm). On the reverse of the mandala, tie your yarn to the long tail that you left out a few wraps back.

* Flip the mandala back over to check the front and make small adjustments with your fingernail, moving yarn strings left or right to make a straight line where the yarn wraps cross over each other along each dowel. This will help center and balance the mandala.

* Once you are done, I recommend that you place a small amount of glue along the back and on the tip of each dowel to ensure that the yarn does not move over time. It is also a nice touch to paint the ends of your sticks black, dark brown, or a color that matches the last color you used. This is optional, and I did not do it for this book, so you may see a glimpse of the wood at the end of my dowels.

ADDING EMBROIDERY

Embroidery work is one last chance to balance the color of your mandala. I often embroider with white yarn around the border to mirror the white used in the center. White also adds a lightness to the outside of the mandala and helps guide the eye to the center. You may also consider using a color you used toward the center of your mandala to help carry it to the outer edges.

These are my top tips for trouble-free embroidery:

* Measure out a length of yarn that will be long enough to complete your design. I find that for a larger embroidery design, if you measure the yarn to two lengths of the mandala's width, that is typically enough for a design on one panel. For a smaller pattern, such as an arrow or triangle, one length of the mandala is plenty.

* Use a tapestry needle that has a large eye so that it is easy to get the yarn through.

* Play around with different designs you like on one of the panels before committing to what you'll do for all the panels.

* Once you get to the end of your design, thread the tail of the yarn back under the blocks of embroidery. If the tail at the end will reach the one at the beginning, tie them together. If they don't, don't worry about it – just thread them under the embroidery to secure them. For extra stability, you may add a touch of glue to keep the yarn tails in place. I also recommend putting a dot of glue on each knot to ensure that it doesn't slip over time.

Contents

YARN MANDALAS
For Beginners & Beyond

Woven wall hangings
for mindful making

INGA SAVAGE

DAVID & CHARLES

www.davidandcharles.com

YARN MANDALAS
For Beginners & Beyond